Matin Latin II

TEACHER'S EDITION

by Karen L. Craig

Illustrated by Laura L. Blakey

Canon Press

MOSCOW, IDAHO

Special Thanks to Charles, Darol, and David
without whose loving encouragement this project would not have been possible,
to Tabithah for practical help,
to Ron and Carol for hospitality,
to the administration at Logos School
for the opportunity to spend time writing these texts.

Karen L. Craig, *Matin Latin 2 (Teacher's Edition)*

©1999 by Karen L. Craig
Published by Canon Press, P.O. Box 8741, Moscow, ID 83843
800-488-2034

Illustrations by Laura L. Blakey
Cover Design by Paige Atwood Design, Moscow, ID

Printed in the United States of America

ISBN: 1-885767-49-8

This book is dedicated to
Doug and Nancy with thanksgiving for their godly example.

Table of Contents

Preface 9

God, gods, goddesses, and myths 10

Suggested Memory Work 11

Pronunciation 13

Lesson One: *Nouns (Review)* 15

   Lesson One Exercises 17

Lesson Two: *Verbs (Review)* 21

   Lesson Two Exercises 22

Lesson Three: *Verb Tenses (Review)* 25

   Lesson Three Exercises 28

Lesson Four: *Adjectives, Prepositions (Review)* 32

   Lesson Four Exercises 33

Lesson Five: *Nouns – Second Declension Masculine* 37

   Lesson Five Exercises 39

Lesson Six: *Nouns – Second Declension Neuter* 43

   Lesson Six Exercises 44

Lesson Seven: *Dative with Adjectives* 49

   Lesson Seven Exercises 52

Optional Unit – Numbers 58

Lesson Eight: *Adverbs – English* 60

   Lesson Eight Exercises 61

Lesson Nine: *Adverbs – Latin* 64

   Lesson Nine Exercises 65

Lesson Ten: *Possessive Pronouns – English and Latin* 69

   Lesson Ten Exercises 71

Lesson Eleven: *Questions* 73

   Lesson Eleven Exercises 74

Lesson Twelve: *Perfect Tense – English* 77

   Lesson Twelve Exercises 79

Lesson Thirteen: *Perfect Tense – Latin* 81

   Lesson Thirteen Exercises 83

Lesson Fourteen: *Conjunctions – Latin* 89

   Lesson Fourteen Exercises 90

Lesson Fifteen: *Pluperfect Tense – English and Latin* 92
    Lesson Fifteen Exercises 93
Lesson Sixteen: *Future Perfect Tense – Latin* 100
    Lesson Sixteen Exercises 102
Lesson Seventeen: *Verbs – Synopsis* 106
    Lesson Seventeen Exercises 107
Lesson Eighteen: *Second Conjugation – Present System* 108
    Lesson Eighteen Exercises 109
Lesson Nineteen: *Second Conjugation – Perfect System* 113
    Lesson Nineteen Exercises 115
Optional Unit – Stories 120
Lesson Twenty: *Nouns – Third Declension* 122
    Lesson Twenty Exercises 125
Lesson Twenty-One: *Third Declension – I-stem* 131
    Lesson Twenty-One Exercises 133
Lesson Twenty-Two: *Irregular Verb – Possum* 136
    Lesson Twenty-Two Exercises 137
Optional Unit – Seasons and Weather 141
Lesson Twenty-Three: *Vocabulary Builder* 143
    Lesson Twenty-Three Exercises 144
Lesson Twenty-Four: *Third Conjugation – Present System* 150
    Lesson Twenty-Four Exercises 152
Lesson Twenty-Five: *Third Conjugation – Perfect System* 155
    Lesson Twenty-Five Exercises 157
Lesson Twenty-Six: *Third Conjugation – I-stem* 158
    Lesson Twenty-Six Exercises 159
Optional Unit – Animals 165
Optional Unit – Animals Exercises 166
Paradigm Summaries 168
Latin Vocabulary 182
Appendix: Patterns for Diagraming Sentences 203

Matin Latin II

Preface

By choosing to study a second year of Latin you've indicated that the question "Why Latin?" has already been settled in your mind. You've seen, or are convinced of, the benefits of logical thinking skills, problem solving ability, vocabulary development, and syntax building. The challenge is to pass along the enjoyment of practical application of these benefits to your students. If Latin is merely another class in your daily schedule, students will develop a tolerance for that period of the day. Some will endure the time more cheerfully than others. However, if skills learned in other classes are used in Latin and skills learned in Latin are brought to other classes or better yet, into daily living, the time spent in the Latin text will be perceived as useful and may even come to be anticipated!

Mathematical skills may be reinforced in Latin study. Learning vocabulary is drill work quite similar to learning addition and multiplication facts. Reading or writing a Latin sentence closely resembles solving an equation for x, y, or z. Sometimes a Latin sentence will appear as a jigsaw puzzle. Music skills may be applied to learning the paradigms. The artistic side of life may be enhanced by encouraging students to picture the Latin story, the same as they would picture a story they read in English. Reading comprehension will be as much a part of Latin readings as it is of English readings. Original composition is the best method available for reviewing vocabulary and case and verb endings. Memorizing Latin poetry or scripture texts will sharpen the mind and create a storehouse of phrases for later use.

The exercises in this text have been written for variety. They certainly do not present an exhaustive resource for reviewing each lesson. By using several types of review tools or pattern drills, find the ones which best meet your students' needs and modify other drills to mimic the best ones for your students. *Beware* of the pitfall of verbatim translation. Although I have laboriously provided direct translations for the grammatical benefit of a deciphering teacher, the word-for-word method will slow down the pace of reading to a boring one at best and a time-consuming endurance contest at worst. Read sentence by sentence, paragraph by paragraph as you do in English. Then to reinforce grammar and to study style and syntax, go back over the selection at another time to parse the reading.

The beauty of language is that it is not simply mathematical, although Latin is very organized, but that there are musical qualities in the rhythm and flow of words and artistic qualities in the meanings and nuances associated with the choice of words. As you and your students become more familiar with the structure and vocabulary of Latin and English, may this new knowledge free you to express your ideas with a clarity unavailable to you before.

God, gods, goddesses, and myths

Nearly every people-group has a set of myths which mirror, although always with distortion, the biblical accounts of creation, the Flood, and natural phenomena in our world. The Sumerians' *Epic of Gilgamesh*, the Greek and Roman myths, Native American folklore, and African tales all attempt to explain the history of the world. Including some study of mythology gives background information about the culture and thought processes of a society. Even young students quickly distinguish between the facts of Scripture and the contrived explanations of storytellers blinded by godlessness (cf. I Chronicles 16:23–30).

As for the myriad gods and goddesses the Romans worshipped, even they may be explained from a study of Scripture. Many scholars believe that the "sons of God" in Genesis 6:1–4 were created beings whose offspring had superhuman characteristics and abilities. The Romans had no trouble accepting Romulus and Remus, founders of Rome, as having been twin sons of a Vestal Virgin, sired by the god Mars.

Throughout Scripture there are several instances of celestial or angelic beings participating in the affairs of men. Worshippers of the true God are distinguished from worshippers of idols, or false gods. The pagans believed that when they warred, their gods warred with them.[1] (See also I Samuel 4:1–10 and I Chronicles 10:8–14.) In Daniel 10:12–14, the archangel Michael, spoken of as a chief prince, came to the aid of the unnamed lesser being who was also supernatural according to the description in verses 1-10. These two had a conflict with the "prince of the kingdom of Persia" (vss. 13, 20). Throughout the rest of the chapter, Daniel is helped by beings like men in appearance, but with superhuman abilities (Dan.10:15–21).

According to Ezekiel 28:1-19, the prince of Tyre and king of Tyre have set themselves against God and proclaimed themselves to be gods. Verses 15–19 make it clear that this being (king of Tyre from v. 12) was created and perfect (a supernatural characteristic) for a time. The word "cherub" refers to a "griffon," a terrifying-looking creature.[2] Psalm 86:8–10 indicates that David accepted the idea of many gods but only one true God. I Chronicles 16:26 distinguishes between the gods of the people and the Lord who made the heavens and all the beings in them.

In the light of Scriptural truth, the myths of ancient peoples appear as the cheap imitations they are. Although one would not wallow in a study of the immoral deeds of these characters—gods, goddesses, demigods, or heathen men—these stories present valuable insights into the lives and thoughts of the people whose language (method of communication) one desires to comprehend.

[1] From *Savior of the World: A Series on Historical Optimism #2*, a sermon by Douglas Wilson, May 25, 1997.
[2] Ibid.

Suggested Memory Work

From Psalm 7

7:2 Domine Deus meus in te speravi salvum me fac ex omnibus persequentibus me et libera me

7:3 nequando rapiat ut leo animam meam dum non est qui redimat neque qui salvum faciat

7:4 Domine Deus meus si feci istud si est iniquitas in manibus meis

7:5 si reddidi retribuentibus mihi mala decidam merito ab inimicis meis inanis

7:6 persequatur inimicus animam meam et conprehendat et conculcet in terra vitam meam et gloriam meam in pulverem deducat diapsalma

From Psalm 19

18:2 caeli enarrant gloriam Dei et opera manuum eius adnuntiat firmamentum

18:3 dies diei eructat verbum et nox nocti indicat scientiam

18:4 non sunt loquellae neque sermones quorum non audiantur voces eorum

18:5 in omnem terram exivit sonus eorum et in fines orbis terrae verba eorum

18:6 in sole posuit tabernaculum suum et ipse tamquam sponsus procedens de thalamo suo exultavit ut gigans ad currendam viam suam;

18:7 a summo caeli egressio eius et occursus eius usque ad summum eius nec est qui se abscondat a calore eius

18:8 lex Domini inmaculata convertens animas testimonium Domini fidele sapientiam praestans parvulis

18:9 iustitiae Domini rectae laetificantes corda praeceptum Domini lucidum inluminans oculos

18:10 timor Domini sanctus permanens in saeculum saeculi iudicia Domini vera iustificata in semet ipsa

18:11 desiderabilia super aurum et lapidem pretiosum multum et dulciora super mel et favum

18:12 etenim servus tuus custodit ea in custodiendis illisretributio multa

18:13 delicta quis intellegit ab occultis meis munda me

18:14 et ab alienis parce servo tuo si mei non fuerint dominati tunc inmaculatus ero et emundabor a delicto maximo

18:15 et erunt ut conplaceant eloquia oris mei et meditatio cordis mei in conspectu tuo semper Domine adiutor meus et redemptor meus cordis mei in conspectu tuo semper Domine adiutor meus et redemptor meus

Selections taken from the Textus Vulgatae Clementinae, the Latin translation of the Holy Bible, commonly known as the Vulgate.

Psalm 23

22:1 psalmus David Dominus reget me et nihil mihi deerit
22:2 in loco pascuae ibi; me conlocavit super aquam refectionis
educavit me
22:3 animam meam convertit deduxit me super semitas iustitiae
propter nomen suum
22:4 nam et si ambulavero in medio umbrae mortis non timebo mala
quoniam tu mecum es virga tua et baculus tuus ipsa me consolata
sunt
22:5 parasti in conspectu meo mensam adversus eos qui tribulant
me inpinguasti in oleo caput meum et calix meus inebrians quam
praeclarus est
22:6 et misericordia tua subsequitur me omnibus diebus vitae
meae et ut inhabitem in domo Domini in longitudinem dierum

Psalm 24

23:1 psalmus David prima sabbati Domini est terra et plenitudo
eius orbis terrarum et universi; qui habitant in eo
23:2 quia; ipse super maria fundavit eum et super flumina
praeparavit eum
23:3 quis ascendit in montem Domini aut quis stabit in loco
sancto eius
23:4 innocens manibus et mundo corde qui non accepit in vano
animam suam nec iuravit in dolo proximo suo
23:5 hic accipiet benedictionem a Domino et misericordiam a Deo
salvatore suo
23:6 haec est generatio quaerentium eum quaerentium faciem Dei
Iacob diapsalma
23:7 adtollite portas principes vestras et elevamini portae
aeternales et introibit rex gloriae
23:8 quis est iste rex gloriae Dominus fortis et potens Dominus
potens in proelio
23:9 adtollite portas principes vestras et elevamini portae
aeternales et introibit rex gloriae
23:10 quis est iste rex gloriae Dominus virtutum ipse est rex
gloriae diapsalma

An alphabetic phonics chart looks like this (to alleviate pronunciation difficulties, in the English examples phonetic symbols from Webster's New Collegiate Dictionary were used):

Vowels					
Long	**Latin**	**English**	**Short**	**Latin**	**English**
ā	irāta, lāta	father	a	casa	banana, but
ē	poēta, rēs, tē	date, day, they	e	et, est	bet, met
ī	prīma, vīlla	beet, easy	i	in, inter	in, pin
ō	Rōma, sōla	bone, no	o	bona, nova	obey, omit
(ō and o are very similar)					
ū	fortūna, lacūna	food, loot, lute	u	sub, sunt	foot, full, put
Diphthongs					
ae	puellae, tubae	aisle, eye			
au	aut, nauta	out, pouch			
(Infrequent dipthongs are included here only for reference: **ei** as in n**ei**ghbor and w**ei**gh; **oe** as in **oy** in b**oy**, j**oy**; **eu** as in f**eu**d, and f**ew**; **ui** as in q**u**een.)					

Consonants			
b, d, f, h, k, l, m, n, p, qu, r sound the same in Latin and in English		s	as in *say*
bs and **bt**	have a soft sound like *ps* and *pt*	t	as in *ton*
c and **ch**	always hard as in *character*	th	as in *thyme* or *thick* (not as in *then*)
g	always hard as in *go*	ti	as in *tin* (does **not** combine as in *nation*)
gu	as in *anguish*	v	always sounds like *w* as in *wall*
i (j)	begins a word and is followed by a vowel; sounds like *y* in *yam*	x	always sounds like *ks* as in *axe* (double consonant)
ph	as in *photograph*	z	always sounds like *dz* as in *adze* (double consonant)

The syllabification of Latin words

Dividing into syllables and placing an accent makes a word easier to pronounce.

A. Each vowel or diphthong has its own syllable.

B. Consonants are pronounced with the following vowel. Two consonants are divided and one pronounced with each vowel.

C. Consonant blends: *h, l,* and *r* combine with a preceding *c, g, p, b, d,* or *t* to form a blend which is pronounced with the following vowel.

D. When *u* follows *g, q,* and sometimes *s,* it sounds like *w* and forms a blend which is pronounced with the following vowel.

E. Double consonants: *x* is pronounced with the preceding vowel, *z* is pronounced with the following vowel.

F. The last syllable of a Latin word is the *ultima,* the next to last is the *penult,* and the one before that is the *antepenult.*

Accents

In words of more than one syllable, the ultima is never accented. (*This rule is ignored during Practice Chants.*) If the penult is long (it has a long vowel or is followed by two or more consonants), it is accented. If the penult is short, the accent will be on the antepenult. Simply stated, *if the next to last syllable is long, it is accented. If the next to last syllable is short, the syllable which precedes it receives the accent.*

Lesson One

In this lesson we will review the noun cases which we have already learned.

A noun is the name of a person, place, thing, or idea. *Girl, boy, forest, water,* and *friendship* are all nouns. Can you name some other nouns? Nouns which tell who or what is doing the action of the sentence are called *subject* nouns, or the *subject* of the sentence. In Latin the subject of a sentence uses the nominative case.

English has cases, too. They are most easily seen with third person pronouns.

Subjective Case: he

Possessive Case: his

Objective Case: him

Example: He saw him and his hat.

In this sentence, *he* is the subject, *him* is the direct object, and *his* shows possession.

There are no articles (a, an, the) in Latin.

A predicate nominative renames the subject after a linking verb. A predicate nominative also uses the nominative case.

A noun which shows possession (the *girl's* coat) uses the genitive case in Latin.

A noun which shows *to whom* or *for whom* the action of the verb was done is called the indirect object. In Latin the indirect object uses the dative case.

A noun which receives the action of a verb is the direct object. In Latin a direct object uses the accusative case.

A noun which is the object of a preposition uses the accusative or the ablative case in Latin. The case of this noun depends on the preposition and the meaning in the sentence.

CASE	SINGULAR	PLURAL
Nominative	puella	puellae
Genitive	puellae	puellārum
Dative	puellae	puellīs
Accusative	puellam	puellās
Ablative	puellā	puellīs

Teacher's Note: Students may find it helpful to highlight the declension endings. It is always best, however, to chant the paradigm using an entire noun, not simply the endings.

Lesson One Exercises

A. Underline the subject in these sentences.

1. The boys sail.

2. The slaves walk.

3. Men call.

4. Horses work.

5. A messenger tells.

6. Agricolae ambulant.

7. Poēta nārrat.

8. Nautae nāvigābant.

9. Famulae labōrābit.

10. Bēstiae vocābant.

1. The <u>boys</u> sail.
2. The <u>slaves</u> walk.
3. <u>Men</u> call.
4. <u>Horses</u> work.
5. A <u>messenger</u> tells.
6. <u>Agricolae</u> ambulant.
7. <u>Poēta</u> nārrat.
8. <u>Nautae</u> nāvigābant.
9. <u>Famulae</u> labōrābit.
10. <u>Bēstiae</u> vocābant.

B. Underline the predicate nominative and circle the direct object in these sentences.

1. Fido is a puppy.

2. The owl caught a mouse.

3. The puppy has a bone.

4. My cat is a Persian.

5. The cow eats corn.

6. Unda nāviculam portat.

7. Fīlia fēmina est.

1. Fido is a <u>puppy</u>.
2. The owl caught a (mouse).
3. The puppy has a (bone).
4. My cat is a <u>Persian</u>.
5. The cow eats (corn).
6. Unda (nāviculam) portat.
7. Fīlia <u>fēmina</u> est.

8. Umbrae ursam cēlābant.

9. Silva cūrās ēvocat.

10. Figūrae deae sunt.

8. Umbrae (ursam) cēlābant.

9. Silva (cūrās) ēvocat.

10. Figūrae <u>deae</u> sunt.

C. Circle the indirect object and underline phrases (groups of words) which show possession. Some sentences will not be marked.

1. God gave Adam a garden.

2. Adam's garden gave Adam and Eve fruit.

3. God told Adam the rules of the garden.

4. Adam obeyed God's rules for a time.

5. Then the serpent told Eve a lie.

6. Bēstia fēminae fābulam dabat.

7. Fābula bēstiae fāma mala erat.

8. Fēmina bēstiam nōn culpābat.

9. Tum fēmina herbam dēsīderābat.

10. Deus (God) fēminae poenam nārrat.

1. God gave (Adam) a garden.

2. <u>Adam's</u> garden gave (Adam and Eve) fruit.

3. God told (Adam) the rules <u>of the garden</u>.

4. Adam obeyed <u>God's</u> rules for a time.

5. Then the serpent told (Eve) a lie.

6. Bēstia (fēminae) fābulam dabat.

7. Fābula <u>bēstiae</u> fāma mala erat.

8. Fēmina bēstiam nōn culpābat.

9. Tum fēmina herbam dēsīderābat.

10. Deus (God) (fēminae) poenam nārrat.

D. Tell the object of the preposition. For the Latin sentences tell the case of the noun.

1. Galba and Silvanus are walking on the seashore.
2. Today the waves are quiet, but pirates are on a nearby island.
3. Galba lives near the coast.
4. Silvanus is a farmer and does not live near the sea.
5. His villa is near high Aetna.
6. Galba vīllam prope Aetnam spectat et fābulam nārrat.
7. "Olim ambulābam in ōrā.
8. Pīrātās cum gemmīs spectābam.
9. Pīrātae in terrā gemmās cēlābant.
10. Tum pīrātās in ōrā nōn dēsīderō!"

---

1. Galba and Silvanus are walking on the *seashore*.
2. Today the waves are quiet, but pirates are on a nearby *island*.
3. Galba lives near the *coast*.
4. Silvanus is a farmer and does not live near the *sea*.
5. His villa is near high *Aetna*.
6. Galba vīllam prope *Aetnam (accusative)* spectat et fābulam nārrat.
7. "Olim ambulābam in *ōrā (ablative)*.
8. Pīrātās cum *gemmīs (ablative)* spectābam.
9. Pīrātae in *terrā (ablative)* gemmās cēlābant.
10. Tum pīrātās in *ōrā (ablative)* nōn dēsīderō!"

E. Review the Latin noun vocabulary from Book One.

DAILY ORAL REVIEW

Complete these sentences:

A noun is

A pronoun takes the place of

A predicate nominative renames

An indirect object shows

A direct object

A noun is *the name of a person, place, or thing (or idea)*.

A pronoun takes the place of *a noun*.

A predicate nominative renames *the subject (after a linking verb.)*

An indirect object shows *to whom* or *for whom* the action of the verb was done.

A direct object *receives the action of a verb*.

Teacher's Note: The daily review for each lesson should be carried into the next lesson as a part of the weekly review. Rote memory of facts combined with the practical application of those facts through the lesson exercises will give the students confidence to be quick and accurate in their work.

Lesson Two

Verbs tell the action of the subject. Verbs have tense—the time that the action happened.

The present tense tells that the action is happening now.

The imperfect tense tells what used to happen or was happening over a long period of time before now.

The future tense tells what will happen in the future, sometime after right now.

Action verbs may have a pronoun (I, you, he, she, it; we, you, they) for a subject. They may also have a direct object.

Linking verbs are different. They do not tell action. They link two parts of the sentence that are the same. A linking verb has a subject and a predicate nominative or a predicate adjective. A linking verb is also called a "state of being verb." The forms of "to be," *is, are, was, were, will be* are easy to identify. Other verbs like *seems, appears, looks,* are also linking verbs.

The infinitive is also a special kind of verb. *To* plus a verb is called the *infinitive*. *To play, to run,* and *to be* are all infinitives.

A mental image may be helpful to the students. An action verb (V) almost always involves movement. A linking verb (LV), or state of being verb, has results which do not require movement. A linking verb almost always has a complement (predicate noun or predicate adjective). An action verb does not necessarily need a complement (direct object).

For example: If a crop grows, *grows* is an action verb; but if a boy grows calm, *grows* is a linking verb. He feels (V) the peach; or the peach feels (LV) fuzzy.

Other linking verbs are *become, look, smell, sound, stay, taste.* If a form of *is* may be substituted for the verb, it is usually a linking verb.

Lesson Two Exercises

A. Label the verb P(Present), I(Imperfect), or F(Future) to show the tense.

_____ 1. Long ago, many men were doing bad deeds.

_____ 2. Noah is a good man.

_____ 3. Noah will build a huge boat for his family.

_____ 4. His family is helping Noah with the ark.

_____ 5. It was taking a long time to build.

_____ 6. Noe et familia in arcā habitant.

_____ 7. Multae aquae in terrā erunt.

_____ 8. Tum multae undae super terram arcam portābant.

_____ 9. Arca super undās et aquās familiam conservābit.

_____ 10. Nunc vīta in terrā nōn erat, sed Noe et familia in
terrā habitābant.

_I__ 1. Long ago, many men were doing bad deeds.

_P__ 2. Noah is a good man.

_F__ 3. Noah will build a huge boat for his family.

_P__ 4. His family is helping Noah with the ark.

_I__ 5. It was taking a long time to build.

_P__ 6. Noe et familia in arcā habitant.

_F__ 7. Multae aquae in terrā erunt.

_I__ 8. Tum multae undae super terram arcam portābant.

_F__ 9. Arca super undās et aquās familiam conservābit.

_I__ 10. Nunc vīta in terrā nōn erat, sed Noe et familia in terrā habitābant.

B. Underline the action verbs, circle the linking verbs, and draw a box around the infinitives. Some sentences have more than one verb.

1. Noah and his sons were the fathers of all people on the earth.

2. Everyone spoke the same language.

3. Many people lived on a plain in the land of Shinar.

4. They decided to build a tower to reach the sky.

5. God was not pleased when he saw the tower.

6. He gave the people many different languages.

7. They did not understand each other.

8. They stopped the building of the tower.

9. Then they found others who spoke their language.

10. Each group moved away to different parts of the earth.

---

1. Noah and his sons (were) the fathers of all people on the earth.

2. Everyone <u>spoke</u> the same language.

3. Many people <u>lived</u> on a plain in the land of Shinar.

4. They <u>decided</u> [to build] a tower [to reach] the sky.

5. God (was) not pleased when he <u>saw</u> the tower.

6. He <u>gave</u> the people many different languages.

7. They <u>did</u> not <u>understand</u> each other.

8. They <u>stopped</u> the building of the tower.

9. Then they <u>found</u> others who <u>spoke</u> their language.

10. Each group <u>moved</u> away to different parts of the earth.

C. Review the Latin verb vocabulary from Book One.

Lesson Three

Latin verbs have four principal parts. The first principal part tells the first person, present form. The second principal part is the infinitive. When it is used by itself it means "*to* plus a verb." But more importantly, this principal part is used to form the three simple tenses (present, imperfect, future) of a verb.

> Infinitive − *re* = present stem

> Present tense = present stem + personal endings

Present

SINGULAR		PLURAL	
vocō	I call	vocā*mus*	we call
vocā*s*	you call	vocā*tis*	you (pl.) call
voca*t*	he, she, it calls	voca*nt*	they call

Imperfect tense =
present stem + tense sign + personal endings

IMPERFECT

vocā*bam*	I was calling	vocā*bāmus*	we were calling
vocā*bās*	you were calling	vocā*bātis*	you were calling
vocā*bat*	he, she, it was calling	vocā*bant*	they were calling

---

Future tense =
present stem + tense sign + personal endings

FUTURE

vocā*bō*	I will call	vocā*bimus*	we will call
vocā*bis*	you will call	vocā*bitis*	you will call
vocā*bit*	he, she, it will call	vocā*bunt*	they will call

Review the verb *sum* in the present, imperfect, and future tenses.

PRESENT

sum	I am	*sumus*	we are
es	you are	*estis*	you (pl.) are
est	he, she, it is	*sunt*	they are

IMPERFECT

eram	I was	*erāmus*	we were
erās	you were	*erātis*	you (pl.) were
erat	he, she, it was	*erant*	they were

FUTURE

erō	I will be	*erimus*	we will be
eris	you will be	*eritis*	you (pl.) will be
erit	he, she, it will be	*erunt*	they will be

Lesson Three Exercises

A. Write the correct Latin verb.

1. amō: 1st person, singular, present tense _____

2. ambulō: 2nd person, plural, imperfect _____

3. cēlō: 3rd person, singular, future _____

4. clāmō: 1st person, plural, imperfect _____

5. errō: 3rd person, plural, present _____

6. sum: 1st person, plural, imperfect _____

7. iuvō: 2nd person, singular, future _____

8. laudō: 2nd person, plural, present _____

9. nāvigō: 3rd person, singular, future _____

10. sum: 2nd person, singular, present _____

1. amō	6. erāmus
2. ambulābātis	7. iuvābis
3. cēlābit	8. laudātis
4. clāmābāmus	9. nāvigābit
5. errant	10. es

B. Tell the English subject pronoun for each of the verbs in exercise A.

1. I	6. we
2. you (pl.)	7. you
3. he, she, it	8. you (pl.)
4. we	9. he, she, it
5. they	10. you

C. Rewrite this paragraph using all future tense verbs. Do not change *inquit* or *inquiunt*.

Ad nautārum casās properat. Nautārum fīliae perterritae, "Cum pīrātīs," inquiunt, "est Iūlia tua." Magna est īra agricolae. Galeam et hastam raptat. Nautae nāviculam suam agricolae dant. Nautae quoque galeās et hastās raptant, et cum agricolā ad pīrātārum nāviculam properant. Tum agricola pīrātās vocat, "Ubi," inquit, "est fīlia mea?" Pīrātae, "Fīlia tua," inquiunt, "in nāviculā nostrā est." Tum agricola pecūniam multam pīrātīs dat. Pīrātae Iūliam ad agricolae nāviculam portant.

Ad nautārum casās *properābit*. Nautārum fīliae perterritae, "Cum pīrātīs," inquiunt, *"erit* Iūlia tua." Magna *erit* īra agricolae. Galeam et hastam *raptābit*. Nautae nāviculam suam agricolae *dabunt*. Nautae quoque galeās et hastās *raptābunt*, et cum agricolā ad pīrātārum nāviculam *properābunt*. Tum agricola pīrātās *vocābit*; "Ubi," inquit, *"erit* fīlia mea?" Pīrātae, "Fīlia tua," inquiunt, "in nāviculā nostrā *erit*." Tum agricola pecūniam multam pīrātīs *dabit*. Pīrātae Iūliam ad agricolae nāviculam *portābunt*.

D. Review the Latin verbs from Book One.

E. Study these new Latin words.

īra, -ae, f.   porta, -ae, f.   properō, -āre, -āvī, -ātum

cēna, -ae, f.	supper
tabula, -ae, f.	tablet
tunica, -ae, f.	tunic
exclāmō, -āre, -āvī, -ātum	to exclaim, to cry out
raptō, -āre, -āvī, -ātum	to snatch, to seize
recitō, -āre, -āvī, -ātum	to read aloud, to recite

DAILY ORAL REVIEW

Chant the noun paradigm using a different noun each day.

Conjugate a verb in the present, imperfect, and future tenses.

By this time in the student's study of Latin, the grammatical forms are established and more emphasis may be placed on building vocabulary, both English and Latin. It is always helpful to point out obvious English derivatives of the weekly vocabulary words. Depending upon the age of the students and the emphasis of the class, a teacher may wish to assign listing English derivatives as part of learning the Latin vocabulary.

For example, from the Latin noun *īra*, we get the English words *ire, irate, ireful, irately, irateness*!

From *porta*: *port* (as in porthole) and *portal*.

From *tabula*: *tabular, tabulate, tabulator*

From *tunica*: *tunic, tunica, tunicate, tunicle*

Older students may be required to know the definitions of some of these English words, as well.

Lesson Four

An adjective modifies (describes) a noun or pronoun.

In Latin an adjective agrees with the noun it modifies in gender, number, and case. So far we have only learned the feminine gender, which is the middle form in a dictionary listing of the adjective.

An adjective answers the questions
which one?, what kind?, how many?
about a noun or pronoun.

A preposition is a short word which tells the relationship of a noun to other parts of the sentence. In book one we learned about Prep, the frog, and his position in relation to his box. He could be *in* the box, *on* the box, *over* the box, etc.

Lesson Four Exercises

A. Underline the adjectives. Draw an arrow to the noun which is being modified.

1. Abraham was an old man who served God.

2. He wanted his only son, Isaac, to have a good wife.

3. He sent his servant Eliezer to find a lovely wife.

4. Eliezer and several men took ten camels to Nahor, a distant country.

5. The tired, thirsty camels knelt beside a deep well of cool water.

6. Puella pulchra aquam portat.

7. Eliezer aquam grātam rogābat.

8. Puella pulchra camelīs altīs aquam grātam dabat.

9. Tum Eliezer puellam grātam laudābat.

10. Puella grāta, bona, et pulchra Isaac erit.

---

1. Abraham was an <u>old</u> >man who served God.
2. He wanted <u>his</u> <u>only</u> >son, Isaac, to have a <u>good</u> >wife.
3. He sent his servant Eliezer to find a <u>lovely</u> >wife.
4. Eliezer and <u>several</u> >men took <u>ten</u> >camels to Nahor's land, a <u>distant</u> >country.
5. The <u>tired</u>, <u>thirsty</u> >camels knelt beside a <u>deep</u> >well of <u>cool</u> >water.
6. Puella< <u>pulchra</u> aquam portat.
7. Eliezer aquam <<u>grātam</u> rogābat.
8. Puella <<u>pulchra</u> camelīs< <u>altīs</u> aquam <<u>grātam</u> dabat.
9. Tum Eliezer puellam < <u>grātam</u> laudābat.
10. Puella <<u>grāta</u>, <u>bona</u>, et <u>pulchra</u> Isaac* erit.

*The girl will be (a wife) for Isaac. The Vulgate does not decline all Hebrew names so there is no dative ending to tell that Isaac is the indirect object here.

This story is from the Bible in Genesis 24. By the end of this textbook, students will be able to read the story in Latin from the Vulgate, the Latin translation of the Bible.

B. Study these new adjectives.

extrēmus, extrēma, extrēmum	extreme, farthest
parātus, parāta, parātum	ready, prepared
perterritus, perterrita, perterritum	terrified, frightened
splendidus, splendida, splendidum	splendid

COLORS

albus, alba, album	white
caeruleus, caerulea, caeruleum	blue
croceus, crocea, croceum	orange
flavus, flava, flavum	yellow
fuscus, fusca, fuscum	brown
niger, nigra, nigrum	black
purpureus, purpurea, purpureum	purple
ruber, rubra, rubrum	red

The students will enjoy pointing to various objects around the room and naming their colors, or making Latin labels for their crayons.

C. Give five English derivatives from the Latin adjectives.

Answers will vary: albino, albatross, Nigeria, ruby, splendid, etc.

D. Underline the prepositional phrases (the preposition and the noun or pronoun that follows, plus any words between them). Use a stilum croceum. (A stilus (-ī, m.) is a writing stick.)

1. In a small cottage near a large forest lived a lazy ant.
2. In summer the ant carried food into her house.
3. Near the ant's house lived a lazy grasshopper.
4. He always sang, but he didn't carry food into his house.
5. In winter the ant had food; the grasshopper had no food on his table.
6. Cicāda (grasshopper) ad casam formīcae (ant) volat; januam pulsat.
7. Per fenestram formīca cicādam spectat.
8. "Cibum dēsīderō!" cicāda inquit (says). Per januam clāmat.
9. In mensā formīcae cibum est quod (because) formica labōrābat cum (when) cicāda cantābat.
10. Cicāda quiēta ā casā formīcae volat; nōn iam cantat.

1. <u>In a small cottage</u> <u>near a large forest</u> lived a lazy ant.
2. <u>In summer</u> the ant carried food <u>into her house</u>.
3. <u>Near the ant's house</u> lived a lazy grasshopper.
4. He always sang, but he didn't carry food <u>into his house</u>.
5. <u>In winter</u> the ant had food; the grasshopper had no food.
6. Cicāda (grasshopper) <u>ad casam</u> formīcae (ant) volat; januam pulsat (knocks).
7. <u>Per fenestram</u> formīca cicādam spectat.
8. "Cibum dēsīderō!" cicāda inquit (says). <u>Per januam</u> clāmat.
9. <u>In mensā</u> formīcae cibum est quod (because) formīca labōrābat cum (when) cicāda cantābat.
10. Cicāda quiēta <u>ā casā</u> formīcae volat; nōn iam cantat.

F. Review the Latin prepositions from Book One.

ā, ab (ablative) *away from*
ad (accusative) *to, toward*

circum (accusative) *around*
cum (ablative) *with*

dē (ablative) *concerning, about*
ē, ex (ablative) *away from*

in (accusative) *into*
in (ablative) *in, on*
inter (accusative) *between, among*

per (accusative) *through*
post (accusative) *after, behind*
prō (ablative) *in front of, for, on behalf of*
prope (accusative) *near*

DAILY ORAL REVIEW

Complete these sentences:

An adjective answers the questions

A preposition tells

An adjective answers the questions *which one? what kind? how many?* about a noun.

A preposition tells *the relation of a noun to another part of the sentence.*

Lesson Five

Latin has five noun declensions. We have already learned many first declension nouns. Most of the first declension nouns are feminine in gender.

Now we will learn the second declension noun paradigms. There is a paradigm for the masculine nouns and one for the neuter nouns. These paradigms are very much alike, so they both belong to the second declension.

Here is the second declension masculine noun paradigm.

CASE	SINGULAR	PLURAL
Nominative	amīc*us*	amīc*ī*
Genitive	amīc*ī*	amīc*ōrum*
Dative	amīc*ō*	amīc*īs*
Accusative	amīc*um*	amīc*ōs*
Ablative	amīc*ō*	amīc*īs*

Most second declension masculine nouns end in *-us* in the nominative form. There are a few which end in *-r* or *-er*. These will have the genitive form given in the text listing so that the stem will be easy to find. (*liber, librī*, m.; *magister, magistrī*, m.)

> ## To find the stem of a noun, drop the ending from the genitive singular form.

A few nouns keep the *-e-* of the nominative form (*puer, puerī,* m.; *vesper, vesperī,* m.), but the declension endings are the same as for the *-us* nouns.

Here is the paradigm for words like *puer, puerī, m.–boy.*

CASE	SINGULAR	PLURAL
Nominative	puer	puer*ī*
Genitive	puer*ī*	puer*ōrum*
Dative	puer*ō*	puer*īs*
Accusative	puer*um*	puer*ōs*
Ablative	puer*ō*	puer*īs*

English derivatives of *-r* and *-er* nouns give clues to their Latin stem: library, magistrate, puerile, vespers.

Lesson Five Exercises

A. Study this new vocabulary. Remember to learn the entire Latin entry for each word.

ager, agrī, m.

annus, annī, m.

lūdus, lūdī, m.

magister, magistrī, m.

puer, puerī, m.

amīcus, amīcī, m.	friend
angulus, angulī, m.	corner
iuvencus, iuvencī, m.	bullock
liber, librī, m.	book

B. Chant the second declension masculine paradigm using a different noun each day.

Monday—ager, agrī

Tuesday—lūdus, lūdī

Wednesday—annus, annī

Thursday—magister, magistrī

Friday—angulus, angulī

---

ager, agrī, agrō, agrum, agrō; agrī, agrōrum, agrīs, agrōs, agrīs

lūdus, lūdī, lūdō, lūdum, lūdō; lūdī, lūdōrum, lūdīs, lūdōs, lūdīs

annus, annī, annō, annum, annō; annī, annōrum, annīs, annōs, annīs

magister, magistrī, magistrō, magistrum, magistrō; magistrī, magistrōrum, magistrīs, magistrōs, magistrīs

angulus, angulī, angulō, angulum, angulō; angulī, angulōrum, angulīs, angulōs, angulīs

---

C. Give the Latin word from which we get each English word.

1. agriculture _____

2. amicable _____

3. ludicrous _____

4. library _____

1. ager
2. amicus
3. lūdus
4. liber

5. annual

6. angle

7. magistrate

| 5. annus |
| 6. angulus |
| 7. magister |

_____

_____

_____

Challenge: Use each of these words in a sentence which shows its meaning.

_____

_____

_____

_____

_____

_____

_____

_____

_____

D. Draw pictures or write a good English sentence to show the meaning of these Latin sentences.

1. Puer in angulō stābat.   2. Magister puerō librum dat.

3. Iuvencī nigrī in agrōs errant.   4. Puerī lūdōs amābunt.

5. Magistrī puerīs et puellīs fābulās in lūdum nārrant.

6. Amīcī puerī cum iuvencīs blancīs nōn labōrābunt.

1. The boy was standing in the corner.
2. The teacher gives the boy a book.
3. The black bullocks are wandering into the fields.
4. The boys will like the games.
5. The teachers tell the boys and girls in the school stories.
6. The boy's friends will not work with the white bullocks.

Lesson Six

The declension of second declension neuter nouns looks very much like the masculine nouns' declension. Notice that the nominative and accusative singular are alike and the nominative and accusative plural are alike. Neuter nouns of the second declension end in *-um* in their nominative singular form.

Here is the second declension neuter noun paradigm.

CASE	SINGULAR	PLURAL
Nominative	for*um*	for*a*
Genitive	forī	forōr*um*
Dative	forō	forīs
Accusative	for*um*	for*a*
Ablative	forō	forīs

All neuter nouns in Latin have the same form for both nominative and accusative. The neuter plural forms always end with *-a*.

Lesson Six Exercises

A. Study this new vocabulary. Remember to learn the entire Latin entry for each word.

benignus, benigna, benignum

caelum, caelī, n.

industrius, industria, industrium

dōnum, dōnī, n.

longinquus, longinqua, longinquum

oppidum, oppidī, n.

piger, pigra, pigrum

proelium, proeliī, n.

forum, forī, n.	forum
impavidus, impavida, impavidum	fearless
nullus, nulla, nullum	no, none
plaustrum, plaustrī, n.	wagon
prandium, prandiī, n.	lunch, dinner

Teacher's Note: With your students, find some proverbs that talk about a vir piger!

B. Say or write the chant for:

cēna

ager

donum

cēna, cēnae, cēnae, cēnam, cēnā; cēnae, cēnārum, cēnīs, cēnās, cēnīs

ager, agrī, agrō, agrum, agrō; agrī, agrōrum, agrīs, agrōs, agrīs

donum, donī, donō, donum, donō; dona, donōrum, donīs, dona, donīs

C. Read the story and underline all the second declension nouns.

Laeta est Iūlia quod iterum casam parvam cum agricolā habitat. Sed Iūlia puella duodecim annōrum iam est. Itaque agricola fīliae suae tabulās dat. Pecūniam quoque lūdī magistrō dat. Cotīdiē puella ad lūdum per agrōs ambulat. Multī iuvēncī in agrōs sunt, sed impavida est puella. Tabulās ad lūdum Iūlia portat. In tabulās litterae multae sunt. Lūdī magister Iūliam laudat quod litterās bene cotīdiē recitat. In lūdō multī puerī, multae puellae cum Iūliā sunt. Magister lūdum bene gubernat. Industriīs puerīs magister librōs pulchrōs dat; pigrōs malōsque puerōs nōn laudat sed culpat. Magna est īra magistrī quod puerī pigrī litterās nōn bene recitant. Itaque puerī pigrī in angulīs stant. Multae sunt lacrimae puerōrum malōrum. Itaque puerī industriī sunt et litterās bene recitant. Iūlia prandium ad lūdum cotīdiē portat, quod longa est via. In agrōs prandium est Iūliae* grātum.

Multās fābulās puerīs et puellīs magister benignus in lūdō nārrat nunc dē Britanniā, nunc dē longinquās terrās fābulās nārrat. Grātae puerīs et puellīs sunt fābulae. Nunc igitur in librō nōn sōlum Iūliae sed multīs etiam puerīs et puellīs fābulās nārrō.

---

bene, adv.—well	*nunc*, adv.—now, at this time
cotīdiē, adv.—every day	*igitur*, adv.—therefore
dē, prep. with abl.—down from, concerning, about	
duodecim—twelve	*itaque*, conj.—and so, therefore
etiam, adv.—even, also	*per*, prep. with acc.—through, among
iam, adv.—now, already, by this time	*-que*—and *(attached to the end of a word)*
nōn iam, adv.—no longer	*sōlum*, adv.—only

It is assumed that the student is familiar with the vocabulary list from Book One of this series. If this is not the case, have students keep their own vocabulary notebook in which they enter unfamiliar vocabulary to be learned. The vocabulary from Book One is a part of the dictionary listing at the end of this text.

Laeta est Iūlia quod iterum casam parvam cum agricolā habitat. Sed Iūlia puella duodecim annōrum iam est. Itaque agricola fīliae suae tabulās dat. Pecūniam quoque lūdī magistrō dat. Cotīdiē puella ad lūdum per agrōs ambulat. Multī iuvēncī in agrōs sunt, sed impavida est puella. Tabulās ad lūdum Iūlia portat. In tabulās litterae multae sunt. Lūdī magister Iūliam laudat quod litterās bene cotīdiē recitat. In lūdō multī puerī, multae puellae cum Iūlia sunt. Magister lūdum bene gubernat. Industriīs puerīs magister librōs pulchrōs dat; pigrōs malōsque puerōs nōn laudat sed culpat. Magna est īra magistrī quod puerī pigrī litterās nōn bene recitant. Itaque puerī pigrī in angulīs stant. Multae sunt lacrimae puerōrum malōrum. Itaque puerī industriī sunt et litterās bene recitant. Iūlia prandium ad lūdum cotīdiē portat, quod longa est via. In agrōs prandium est Iūliae grātum.

Multās fābulās puerīs et puellīs magister benignus in lūdō nārrat nunc dē Britanniā, nunc dē longinquās terrās fābulās nārrat. Grātae puerīs et puellīs sunt fābulae. Nunc igitur in librō nōn sōlum Iūliae sed multīs etiam puerīs et puellīs fābulās nārrō.

Julia is happy because she is living again in (her) small cottage with the farmer. But the girl Julia is now twelve years old. Therefore the farmer gives (his) daughter tablets. He also gives money to the teacher of the school. Every day the girl walks to school through the fields. Many bullocks are in the fields, but the girl is fearless. Julia carries the tablets to school. On the tablets are many letters. The teacher of the school praises Julia because she recites her letters well every day. In the school are many boys and many girls with Julia. The teacher governs the school well. To the industrious boys the teacher gives beautiful books; he does not praise, but blames (holds guilty) the wicked and lazy boys. Great is the anger of the teacher because the lazy boys do not recite their letters well. Therefore the lazy boys stand in corners. Many are the tears of the wicked boys. And thus (therefore) the boys are industrious and recite (their) letters well. Julia carries (her) lunch to school every day, because the way is long. Lunch in the fields is pleasing to Julia.

The kind teacher tells many stories to the boys and girls. Now he tells about Britain, now (he tells) stories of faraway lands. The stories are pleasing to the boys and girls. So now in this book I am telling stories not only about Julia, but also about many boys and girls.

D. Answer these questions about the story using good Latin sentences.

1. Why does Julia's father give her tablets?

2. Where does Julia take the tablets?

3. Why is Julia praised?

4. What happens to lazy boys in this school?

5. Why does Julia carry a lunch to school?

6. What kind of stories will be in this book?

---

1. Iūlia duodecim annōrum est.
2. Tabulās ad lūdum portat.
3. Magister Iūliam laudat quod litterās bene cotīdiē recitat.
4. Puerī pigrī in angulīs stant.
5. Iūlia prandium portat quod longa est via.
6. In librō nōn sōlum Iūliae sed multīs etiam puerīs et puellīs fābulās erit.

Lesson Seven

In the story in lesson six, we had a new construction! A *construction* in Latin is the use of a case for a particular reason. Look at these sentences from the story.

In agrīs prandium est Iūliae grātum.

Grātae puerīs et puellīs sunt fābulae.

What case is used for *Iūliae, puerīs,* and *puellīs*? It is the dative case. This use of the dative is called the *dative with adjectives*. With adjectives like *grātus (pleasing), benignus (kind), amīcus (friendly), propinquus (near),* which often carry the meaning *to,* the dative case is used. In the sentences above, the lunch is pleasing (to) Julia; the stories are pleasing (to) the boys and girls.

The story also had many masculine nouns which had adjectives to modify them. Here are some examples.

multī puerī

industriīs puerīs

librōs pulchrōs

puerī pigrī

puerōrum malōrum

How are these adjectives different from the ones we've used before? They have masculine endings because they are modifying masculine nouns.

Adjectives agree with the nouns they modify in gender, number, and case.

Adjectives which modify neuter nouns would have neuter endings. Here are examples of neuter nouns and their adjectives.

oppidum longinquum

magnō forō

nulla dona

prandiīs bonīs

We have learned only two declensions of nouns and adjectives. Therefore many times the ending of an adjective will be the same as the ending of the noun it modifies. *However*, do not rely on this sameness to identify them. An adjective agrees with the noun it modifies in gender, number, and case . . . even when they don't look alike.

Think about how we would talk about a good farmer. What would the nominative noun look like? What would the

Masculine nouns which end in *-ius* in the nominative retain the *-i-* in the stem. Some authors, however, drop the *-i-* in the genitive singular to distinguish it from the nominative plural. In most instances the context will make this distinction.

nominative adjective look like? Would they have the same ending? *Agricola bonus* would be the correct way to write the nominative form. The endings do not *look* alike, but they are the same gender (masculine), number (singular), and case (nominative).

Lesson Seven Exercises

A. Fill in the paradigm for a complete declension of the adjective *bonus*. Some of the spaces have been filled for you.

SINGULAR

	MASCULINE	FEMININE	NEUTER
Nominative	bonus	bona	bonum
Genitive	bonī		
Dative		bonae	
Accusative			bonum
Ablative			

PLURAL

	MASCULINE	FEMININE	NEUTER
Nominative	bonī	bonae	bona
Genitive			bonōrum
Dative		bonīs	
Accusative	bonōs		
Ablative	bonīs		

Singular

	Masculine	Feminine	Neuter
Nominative	bonus	bona	bonum
Genitive	bonī	bonae	bonī
Dative	bonō	bonae	bonō
Accusative	bonum	bonam	bonum
Ablative	bonō	bonā	bonō

Plural

	Masculine	Feminine	Neuter
Nominative	bonī	bonae	bona
Genitive	bonōrum	bonārum	bonōrum
Dative	bonīs	bonīs	bonīs
Accusative	bonōs	bonās	bona
Ablative	bonīs	bonīs	bonīs

B. Decline (orally):

fēmina benigna

magnus angulus

caelum rubrum

nauta impavidus

fēmina benigna, fēminae benignae, fēminae benignae, fēminam benignam, fēminā benignā; fēminae benignae, fēminārum benignārum, fēminīs·benignīs, fēminās benignās, fēminīs benignīs

magnus angulus, magnī angulī, magnō angulō, magnum angulum, magnō angulō; magnī angulī, magnōrum angulōrum, magnīs angulīs, magnōs angulōs, magnīs angulīs

caelum rubrum, caelī rubrī, caelō rubrō, caelum rubrum, caelō rubrō; caela rubra, caelōrum rubrōrum, caelīs rubrīs, caela rubra, caelīs rubrīs

nauta impavidus, nautae impavidī, nautae impavidō, nautam impavidum, nautā impavidō; nautae impavidī, nautārum impavidōrum, nautīs impavidīs, nautās impavidōs, nautīs impavidīs

C. Study this new vocabulary.

aedificō, -āre, -āvī, -ātum	to build
arō, -āre, -āvī, -ātum	to plow
Britannus, Britannī, m.	a Briton
clīvus, clīvī, m.	hill
equus, equī, m.	horse
Italia, Italiae, f.	Italy
Italus, Italī. m.	an Italian
oculus, oculī, m.	eye
olīva, olīvae, f.	olive
oppidānus, oppidānī, m.	townsman
placidus, placida, placidum	calm
rectus, recta, rectum	straight, right
Rōmānus, Rōmāna, Rōmānum *(adj.)*	Roman
ūva, ūvae, f.	grape
validus, valida, validum	strong
vīnea, vīneae, f.	vineyard

D. Use a dictionary, if needed, to find the origin and meaning of these English words.

1. equestrienne _____

2. oculomotor nerve _____

3. vineyard _____

4. edify _____

5. arable _____

---

1. equestrienne—fr. *equus*, a woman who rides on horseback.

2. oculomotor nerve—fr. *oculus*, a nerve which extends from the midbrain to the eyeball and aids in movement of the eyeball.

3. vineyard—fr. *vīnea*, a planting of vines, usually grapevines.

4. edify—fr. *aedificiō*, long ago this word meant "to build." Now it usually means to instruct (for the purpose of improvement) in moral precepts. Related words are *edifice, edification, edificatory*.

5. arable—fr. *arō*, land that is able to be tilled.

E. Read this story.

ITALIA

Caeruleum est Italiae caelum. Italī caelum caeruleum amant. Britannīs quoque caelum caeruleum grātum est, sed nōn saepe Britanniae caelum caeruleum est. Italiae agricolae olivās et ūvās laudant, iuvencīs albīs agrōs arant. Placidī sunt oculī iuvencōrum. Placidī et pulchrī sunt iuvencī. Italiae agricolīs grātī sunt iuvencī. Britannicī agricolae nōn iuvencīs sed equīs agrōs arant. Validī et pulchrī sunt, equī magnī.

In Italiā clīvī multī sunt. Italiā in clīvīs parvīs oppida aedificant. Oppidānī oppida in clīvīs habitant. In campō vīneae et olīvae sunt in clīvīs, oppida. Per campōs viae Rōmānae sunt. Longae et rectae sunt viae Rōmānae. Oppidānī olīvīs et ūvās, agricolae pecūniam dēsīderant. Itaque oppidānī pecūniam agricolīs dant, et per viās Rōmānās agricolae olīvās et ūvās ad oppida in plaustrīs portant.

Italia

Blue is the sky of Italy. The Italians like the blue sky. To the Britons also the blue sky is pleasing, but the sky of Britain is not often blue. The farmers of Italy praise the olives and the vineyards; they plow the fields with white bullocks. Calm are the eyes of the bullocks. Calm and beautiful are the bullocks. The bullocks are pleasing to the farmers of Italy. The British farmers do not plow (their) fields with bullocks but with horses. Strong and beautiful are (their) many horses.

In Italy are many hills. The Italians build towns on the small hills. The townsmen live in towns on the hills. On the plains are vineyards and olives -- on the hills, towns. Through the plains are Roman roads. Long and straight are the Roman roads. The townsmen want olives and grapes; the farmers want money. So the townsmen give the farmers money, and through the Roman roads the farmers carry olives and grapes to the towns in wagons.

F. Draw three pictures from the story above:

1) Show the British farmers in their fields.

2) Show the Italian farmers in their fields.

3) Show the townspeople and the farmers of Italy.

G. Conjugate *saltō* in the present, imperfect, and future tenses.

The students will enjoy doing these practice drills orally. It is also good practice for each student to conjugate a different verb and then exchange papers for checking. Variety in the review routines makes good sense.

Present: saltō, saltās, saltat; saltāmus, saltātis, saltant

Imperfect: saltābam, saltābās, saltābat; saltābāmus, saltābātis, saltābant

Future: saltābō, saltābis, saltābit; saltābimus, saltābitis, saltābunt

DAILY ORAL REVIEW

An adjective agrees with the noun it modifies in gender, number, and case.

Optional Unit – Numbers

Numerals are adjectives; they tell *how many*. Most of them, however, are indeclinable. This makes them quite easy to use in sentences and for daily activities.

The cardinal numerals are the counting numbers. *Unus, duo,* and *trēs* are declined.

The ordinal numerals tell order (first, second, third), and they are declined like *bonus, -a, um*.

Here are the paradigms for *ūnus, duo,* and *trēs*.

	MASCULINE	FEMININE	NEUTER
SINGULAR			
Nominative	ūnus	ūna	ūnum
Genitive	ūnīus	ūnīus	ūnīus
Dative	ūnī	ūnī	ūnī
Accusative	ūnum	ūnam	ūnum
Ablative	ūnō	ūnā	ūnō
PLURAL			
Nominative	duo	duae	duo
Genitive	duōrum	duārum	duōrum
Dative	duōbus	duābus	duōbus
Accusative	duōs	duās	duo
Ablative	duōbus	duābus	duōbus

	MASCULINE/FEMININE	NEUTER
Nominative	trēs	tria
Genitive	trium	trium
Dative	tribus	tribus
Accusative	trēs	tria
Ablative	tribus	tribus

ROMAN NUMERALS

	CARDINAL	ORDINAL
I	ūnus, -a, -um	prīmus
II	duo, duae, duo	secundus
III	trēs, trēs, tria	tertius
IV	quattuor	quārtus
V	quīnque	quīntus
VI	sex	sextus
VII	septem	septimus
VIII	octō	octāvus
IX	novem	nōnus
X	decem	decimus
XI	ūndecim	ūndecimus
XII	duodecim	duodecimus
XIII	tredecem	tertius decimus
XIV	quattuordecim	quārtus decimus
XV	quīndecim	quīntus decimus
XVI	sēdecim	sextus decimus
XVII	septendecim	septimus decimus
XVIII	duodēvīgintī	duodēvīcēsimus
XIX	ūndēvīgintī	ūndēvīcēsimus
XX	vīgintī	vīcēsimus
L	quīnquāgintā	
C	centum	
M	mīlle	

Lesson Eight

In this lesson we will learn another part of a sentence, the adverb. An adverb modifies a verb, an adjective, or another adverb.

An adverb answers the questions
how? when? where? how much?
about a verb, an adjective, or another adverb.

Adverbs in English often (but not always) end in *-ly. Quickly, happily,* and *suddenly* are all adverbs. Words like *high, there,* and *very* are adverbs, too.

> Adverbs *add* meaning *to verbs.*

Sometimes the same word can have different uses in sentences. For example, in the following sentences *high* is used as an adjective or an adverb.

The bear was on a high branch. (adjective)

The high jump bar is missing. (adjective)

The bear is high in the tree. (adverb)

High in the sky is a small cloud. (adverb)

Sometimes we can tell that an adverb was made from an adjective. By adding *-ly* to these adjectives we create adverbs: *slow (slowly), strong (strongly), certain (certainly), sure (surely), loud (loudly), large (largely), near (nearly)*.

Lesson Eight Exercises

A. Underline the adverbs and draw arrows to the words they modify. Use a stilum purpureum.

1. Isaac and Rebekah lived happily together.

2. They greatly desired to have children.

3. Isaac prayed very earnestly to God.

4. Soon Rebekah would have twin sons.

5. Later they would be two great nations.

6. Abraham, the boys' grandfather, lived uprightly and prayerfully.

7. Abraham died and God blessed Isaac richly.

8. Jacob and Esau, Isaac's sons, were quite different.

9. Jacob lived quietly in a tent and his farm was well cared for.

10. Once, Esau hunted until he was very hungry.

11. He looked longingly at the soup Jacob was making.

12. He foolishly sold his birthright for a bowl of soup.

1. Isaac and Rebekah lived <u>happily</u> <u>together</u>.
2. They <u>greatly</u> >desired to have children.
3. Isaac prayed <u>very</u> ><u>earnestly</u> (>prayed) to God.
4. <u>Soon</u> Rebekah >would have twin sons.
5. <u>Later</u> they >would be two great nations.
6. Abraham, the boys' grandfather, lived <<u>uprightly</u> and <u>prayerfully.</u>
7. Abraham died and God blessed< Isaac <u>richly</u>.
8. Jacob and Esau, Isaac's sons, were <u>quite</u> >different.
9. Jacob lived< <u>quietly</u> in a tent and his farm was <u>well</u> (>was cared for).
10. <u>Once</u>, Esau >hunted until he was <u>very</u> >hungry.
11. He looked< <u>longingly</u> at the soup Jacob was making.
12. He <u>foolishly</u> >sold his birthright for a bowl of soup.

B. Tell whether the underlined word is an adjective or an adverb.
Remember: Adjectives tell which one? what kind? how many?
Adverbs tell how? when? where? to what extent? (how much?)
Use a stilum rubrum.

1. He looked <u>thoughtful</u>.

2. The girl gazed <u>thoughtfully</u> at the letter.

3. The price of the dress was very <u>high</u>.

4. Even a child can swing <u>high</u> on this swing!

5. <u>Soon</u> he will be flying.

6. She will be running <u>fast</u>.

7. The <u>fast</u> pitch landed in the catcher's mitt.

8. <u>Happily</u> they walked in the meadow.

9. They were <u>happy</u> to see the king.

10. <u>Now</u> they will live peaceably.

1. adjective
2. adverb
3. adjective
4. adverb
5. adverb
6. adverb
7. adjective
8. adverb
9. adjective
10. adverb

DAILY ORAL REVIEW

An adjective answers the questions *which one? what kind? how many?* about a noun.

An adjective agrees with the noun it modifies in gender, number, and case.

An adverb answers the questions *how? when? where? how much?* about a verb, an adjective, or another adverb.

Lesson Nine

Adverbs in Latin have the same use as in English. They modify verbs, adjectives, and other adverbs. Many times (but not always) Latin adverbs end in -ē.

To form an adverb from a first or second declension adjective, add -ē to the adjective stem.

Adjective stem + ē = adverb

ADJECTIVE

altus   *high, deep*

longus   *long*

miser   *sad, wretched*

pulcher   *beautiful*

ADVERB

altē   *on high, deeply*

longē   *far off, by far*

miserē   *sadly, wretchedly*

pulchrē   *beautifully*

As in English, some adverbs are formed irregularly. *Bonus* becomes *bene*, and *malus* becomes *male.* Other irregular adverbs will be listed as vocabulary entries.

Lesson Nine Exercises

A. Study these new vocabulary words.

cantō, -āre, -āvī, -ātum

deus, -ī, m.

lātus, -a, -um

palla, -ae, f.

vir, virī, m

cicāda, -ae, f.	grasshopper
inter (*acc.*)	between, among
iūcundus, -a, -um	pleasant
lacerta, -ae, f.	lizard
mactō, -āre, -āvī, -ātum	to offer up, to slay, to sacrifice
monumentum, -ī, n.	monument
nōn iam	no longer
ōlim	one day, once upon a time
ruīna, -ae, f.	ruin
templum, -ī, n.	temple
toga, -ae, f.	toga, the robe of a Roman man
undique	on every side, from all sides
victima, -ae, f.	victim

This vocabulary list is longer than usual. However, if the student is encouraged to look for derivatives as an aid in memory, the list will not be unmanagable. *Cicāda, monumentum, ruīna, templum, toga,* and *victima* all have obvious meanings.

B. Read the story. The adverbs are underlined for you.

ROMA

<u>Olim</u> Rōmānī parvum oppidum habitābant. <u>Nunc</u> magna et splendida est Rōma; magnae et lātae sunt viae oppidī. In angulīs viārum rosae sunt; Rōmānī templīs et monumentīs viās ornant. <u>Olim</u> in Forō Rōmānō templa multa et splendida erant. <u>Cotīdiē</u> virī Rōmānī in Forō ambulābant. Albae erant togae virōrum, sed rubrae et caeruleae et croceae erant pallae fēminārum. Arae <u>quoque</u> in Forō erant. In ārīs Rōmānī multās victimās deīs Rōmānīs mactābant. <u>Nōn iam</u> templa sunt in Forō Rōmānō. Nōn iam mactant Rōmānī victimās in ārīs. Sed <u>etiam</u> <u>nunc</u> pulchrum est Forum Rōmānum. Multae sunt ruinae; multae rosae inter ruinās sunt. Inter ruinās et rosās parvae lacertae properant. Pulchrae et iūcundae sunt lacertae. Cicādae <u>quoque</u> <u>undique</u> cantant. Lacertīs et cicādīs grātum est caelum caeruleum.

Rōma, -ae, f.—Rome   *Rōmānus, -ī,* m.—a Roman

Long ago the Romans lived in a small town. Now great and splendid is Rome; great and wide are the roads of the town. In the corners of the roads are roses; the Romans decorate the roads with temples and monuments. Once upon a time there were many and splendid temples in the Roman Forum. Every day the Roman men walked in the Forum. The men's togas were white, but the women's mantles were red and blue and yellow. Altars were in the Forum also. On the altars the Romans offered up many victims to the Roman gods. No longer are temples in the Roman Forum. No longer do the Romans offer victims on the altars. But even now the Roman Forum is beautiful. Many are the ruins; many roses are among the ruins. Among the ruins and the roses hurry small lizards. The lizards are beautiful and pleasant. Grasshoppers also sing from all sides. The blue sky is pleasing to the lizards and grasshoppers.

C. Write an original sentence using the adverb given.

1. placidē _____

_____

2. iūcundē _____

_____

3. lātē _____

_____

4. pulchrē _____

_____

5. sōlum _____

_____

D. Give ten English derivatives from this lesson's vocabulary.

1. _____

2. _____

3. _____

4. _____

5. _____

6. _____

7. _____

8. _____

9. _____

10. _____

This list is certainly not conclusive:

cant, canticle, cantata, chant, deity, interact, interest, interface, interim, interlude, jocund, latitude, monument, ruin, temple, toga, victim, virile, virtue, virtual, virtuosa

Lesson Ten

We have learned that adjectives modify nouns or pronouns, and we have learned to use many adjectives in our writing. Possessive pronouns are a special group of adjectives. They are used to show ownership. In English the possessive pronouns are: *my, mine, your, yours, his, her, hers, its, our, ours, their, theirs.* Study the personal pronouns in these sentences. Notice that they modify a noun, like an adjective does. They answer the adjective question *which one?*

Joshua told the people that Canaan was their *land.*

Joshua prepared his *army for battle.*

Rahab hid spies on her *roof.*

When Jericho was destroyed, Rahab and her *family were safe.*

"Our God is great," Joshua told his *people.*

"Prepare your *hearts to worship."*

In Latin, the possessive pronouns are often omitted when the meaning is clear without them. When they are used, however, they agree with the nouns they modify in gender, number, and case. They look like adjectives.

Here is a chart of the possessive pronouns.

IF THE NOUN BELONGS TO ONE PERSON

1st Person	meus, mea, meum, (*my*)
2nd Person	tuus, tua, tuum, (*your*)
3rd Person	suus, sua, suum, (reflexive . . . *his own*)

IF A NOUN BELONGS TO MORE THAN ONE PERSON

1st Person	noster, nostra, nostrum, (*our*)
2nd Person	vester, vestra, vestrum, (*your*)
3rd Person	suus, sua, suum (reflexive . . . *their own*)

Like any other adjective, a possessive pronoun agrees with the noun it modifies in gender, number, and case. The gender of the owner is not important. Study these examples of possessive pronouns.

Ad patriam nostram *nāvigābimus.*

Cerēs cum fīliā suā *habitābat.*

Patruus meus *fīliam* tuam *ad patriam* suam *portat.*

Ubi est fīlia mea?

Lesson Ten Exercises

A. Decline each of the possessive pronouns we studied in this chapter.

This chant will appear in this order: Masculine, feminine, neuter in case order, singular forms; then plural forms.

meus, mea, meum; meī, meae, meī; meō, meae, meō; meum, meam, meum; meō, meā, meō; meī, meae, mea; meōrum, meārum, meōrum; meīs, meīs, meīs; meōs, meās, mea; meīs, meīs, meīs

tuus, tua, tuum; tuī, tuae, tuī; tuō, tuae, tuō; tuum, tuam, tuum; tuō, tuā, tuō; tuī, tuae, tua; tuōrum, tuārum, tuōrum; tuīs, tuīs, tuīs; tuōs, tuās, tua; tuīs, tuīs, tuīs

suus, sua, suum; suī, suae, suī; suō, suae, suō; suum, suam, suum; suō, suā, suō; suī, suae, sua; suōrum, suārum, suōrum; suīs, suīs, suīs; suōs, suās, sua; suīs, suīs, suīs

noster, nostra, nostrum; nostrī, nostrae, nostrī; nostrō, nostrae, nostrō; nostrum, nostram, nostrum; nostrō, nostrā, nostrō; nostrī, nostrae, nostra; nostrōrum, nostrārum, nostrōrum; nostrīs, nostrīs, nostrīs; nostrōs, nostrās, nostra; nostrīs, nostrīs, nostrīs

vestrus, vestra, vestrum; vestrī, vestrae, vestrī; vestrō, vestrae, vestrō; vestrum, vestram, vestrum; vestrō, vestrā, vestrō; vestrī, vestrae, vestra; vestrōrum, vestrārum, vestrōrum; vestrīs, vestrīs, vestrīs; vestrōs, vestrās, vestra; vestrīs, vestrīs, vestrīs

suus, sua, suum; suī, suae, suī; suō, suae, suō; suum, suam, suum; suō, suā, suō; suī, suae, sua; suōrum, suārum, suōrum; suīs, suīs, suīs; suōs, suās, sua; suīs, suīs, suīs

B. Write ten sentences of your own using possessive pronouns and vocabulary from lessons seven and nine.

1. _____
2. _____
3. _____
4. _____
5. _____
6. _____
7. _____
8. _____
9. _____
10. _____

C. Give an English derivative for each Latin verb.

1. dormītō (to sleep)   _____
2. habeō (to have)   _____
3. lacrimō (to cry)   _____
4. maneō (to stay)   _____
5. sedeō (to sit)   _____

dormitory, habit, lacrimal glands, mansion, sedentation

Lesson Eleven

Being able to write and speak sentences is very important, but sometimes when we communicate we need to ask questions. In Latin there are several ways to ask questions.

We may place the verb at the beginning of a sentence and add *-ne* to it.

> Eratne agricola in agrō?
>
> Portantne plaustrī multās ūvās?
>
> Nārratne famula parvae puellae fābulam?

Sometimes *minimē* (not at all) and *ita* (yes, thus) are used to answer questions instead of a complete sentence.

We may also form questions by using adverbs like *ubi* (where, where from?), *cūr* (why?), *unde* (where to?), and *quandō* (when?)

> Cūr Britannī equīs arābant?
>
> Quandō cēna in mensā erit?
>
> Ubi sum?
>
> Unde ambulābimus?

Lesson Eleven Exercises

A. Ask these questions in Latin. Be courageous! Break the sentence into small parts and work on one part at a time. Find the question word; find the verb; find the subject; find the direct object; find the prepositional phrases. *You can do it!*

    1. Why is the sailor walking into the splendid town?

_____

    2. Where is his small boat?

_____

    3. Is he looking at your beautiful daughter in the field?

_____

    4. Will the wicked pirate carry many red helmets in his ship?

_____

_____

    5. Will the frightened townspeople hurry from the town in
       vain?

_____

_____

    6. From where does the kind and fearless farmer walk?

_____

_____

7. When were the pirates hurrying away from the town?

_____

8. Why are the happy townspeople singing and dancing?

_____

9. Will the sailor and your daughter praise the strong farmer?

_____

_____

10. Were we singing from all sides?

_____

_____

---

1. Cūr nauta in oppidum splendidum ambulat?

2. Ubi nāvicula sua est?

3. Spectatne fīliam pulchram tuam in agrō?

4. Portābitne pīrāta malus multās galeās nāviculā? (ablative of means)

5. Properābuntne oppidānī perterritī ab oppidō frustrā?

6. Ubi agricola benignus et impavidus ambulat?

7. Quandō pīrātae ab oppidō properābant?

8. Cūr oppidānī laetī cantant et saltant?

9. Laudābuntne (plural subject) nauta et fīlia tua agricolam validum?

10. Cantābāmusne undique?

Daily Oral Review

Decline *puella bona*, *puer bonus*, *dōnum bonum*.

Conjugate *vocō* in the present, imperfect, and future tenses.

Conjugate *sum* in the present, imperfect, and future tenses.

---

puella bona, puellae bonae, puellae bonae, puellam bonam, puellā bonā; puellae bonae, puellārum bonārum, puellīs bonīs, puellās bonās, puellīs bonīs

puer bonus, puerī bonī, puerō bonō, puerum bonum, puerō bonō; puerī bonī, puerōrum bonōrum, puerīs bonīs, puerōs bonōs, puerīs bonīs

dōnum bonum, dōnī bonī, dōnō bonō, dōnum bonum, dōnō bonō; dōna bona, dōnōrum bonōrum, dōnīs bonīs, dōna bona, dōnīs bonīs

vocō, vocās, vocat, vocāmus, vocātis, vocant; vocābam, vocābās, vocābat, vocābāmus, vocābātis, vocābant; vocābō, vocābis, vocābit, vocābimus, vocābitis, vocābunt

sum, es, est; sumus, estis, sunt; eram, erās, erat, erāmus, erātis, erant; erō, eris, erit, erimus, eritis, erunt

Lesson Twelve

We have learned three verb tenses, present, perfect, and future. These are sometimes called the present system because in Latin they add tense signs and personal endings to the present stem.

There are three other verb tenses. These are called the perfect tenses because in Latin they add tense signs and personal endings to the perfect stem.

We have been using the imperfect tense to tell of continuing action in the past. The action was not completed all at once.

> Imperfect comes from the Latin words *in* + *perfectus*. In this case, *in* means *not*. So our action was *not perfect*. Children can understand the concept of repeating an action because it was not perfect in contrast to completing the action perfectly on the first try.

Now we will learn about the *perfect tense*, the verb tense which tells about a past action which was done only once or was completed in a short period of time.

\ All Past Times	\ Present /	Future Times /
Perfect Imperfect	Present	Future

< —.———~~~~—]----------[————————————>

In English, this verb tense is expressed by using the past form of the verb (usually identified by the *-ed* ending), or by using *has* or *have* or *did* with the past form of the verb. When *have* or *has* or *did* is used with another verb, it is called a "helping verb" and is counted as part of the verb.

These sentences express completed past action using the perfect tense.

Joseph's family *moved* to Goshen.

Pharoah *has enslaved* Joseph's family.

A princess *adopted* Moses.

The Hebrews *did escape* from Egypt.

Many English verbs have irregular past forms. These verbs do not add *-ed* to show perfect tense action. Because we use these words every day, we do not think of them as *irregular*. Read these sentences which also express the perfect tense.

> Both the imperfect and the perfect tenses may be expressed in English by the *-ed* form of the verb. It is important to maintain an awareness of the distinction in time of these two forms. The imperfect is used for habitual or continuing past action. It is also used for descriptions. (She was a beautiful baby.) The perfect tense is used to express a single completed past action.

He *ran* to the store and home again.

He *has run* to the store.

She *took* seven puppies to the farm.

She *has taken* seven rabbits, too.

Last week, I *saw* a robin.

We *have seen* ten squirrels at one time!

Lesson Twelve Exercise

A. Underline the perfect verbs. Use a stilum fuscum!

1. God gave His people rules for living.

2. The people promised to obey the rules.

3. Moses broke the stone tablet because the people were worshiping a gold calf while he was talking with God.

4. Later, they did follow God's instructions and built a special place to worship Him.

5. God promised His protection for the people as they were traveling in the wilderness.

6. The leaders counted the people before they left Mt. Sinai.

7. The families lined up for the march.

8. Before leaving, each family celebrated the Passover Feast.

9. The people were complaining about having no meat, so God gave them meat and a punishment.

10. Spies reported that Canaan was a good land.

---

1. God <u>gave</u> His people commandments for living.
2. The people <u>promised</u> to obey the rules.
3. Moses <u>broke</u> the stone tablet because the people were worshiping a gold calf while he was talking with God.
4. Later, they <u>did follow</u> God's instructions and <u>built</u> a special place to worship Him.
5. God <u>promised</u> His protection for the people as they were traveling in the wilderness.
6. The leaders <u>counted</u> the people before they <u>left</u> Sinai.
7. The families <u>lined</u> (<u>up</u>) for the march.
8. Before leaving, each family <u>celebrated</u> the Passover Feast.
9. The people were complaining about having no meat, so God <u>gave</u> them meat and a punishment.
10. Spies <u>reported</u> that Canaan was a good land.

B. Underline the perfect verbs, cross out the imperfect verbs. *Do not mark* verbs which are not imperfect or perfect forms.

1. The people complained all the time.

2. Twelve spies scouted in Canaan.

3. Joshua and Caleb said the people should move to this good land.

4. The other ten men, who were not trusting God, were saying that the Canaanites were too tall for the Hebrews to overcome.

5. The earth did swallow one group of disobedient Hebrews.

6. Moses hit a rock instead of speaking to it.

7. Aaron died in the wilderness.

8. The people wandered around and around for forty years.

9. Once, God punished them by sending snakes into camp.

10. Moses prayed and God told him to make a bronze snake on a pole for the people to look at and be healed.

---

1. The people <u>complained</u> all the time.
2. Twelve spies <u>scouted</u> in Canaan.
3. Joshua and Caleb <u>said</u> the people should move to this good land.
4. The other ten men, who ~~were not trusting~~ God, ~~were saying~~ that the Canaanites ~~were~~ too tall for the Hebrews to overcome.
5. The earth <u>did swallow</u> one group of disobedient Hebrews.
6. Moses <u>hit</u> a rock instead of speaking to it.
7. Aaron <u>died</u> in the wilderness.
8. The people <u>wandered</u> around and around for forty years.
9. Once, God <u>punished</u> them by sending snakes into camp.
10. Moses <u>prayed</u> and God <u>told</u> him to make a bronze snake on a pole for the people to look at and be healed.

Lesson Thirteen

In Latin the *perfect tense* is formed by finding the perfect stem of the verb and adding the perfect tense personal endings. This is a special set of endings used only for this tense. To find the perfect stem, think of the third principal part of the verb and take off the *-ī*.

Perfect stem = third principal part - *ī*

Perfect tense = perfect stem + perfect personal endings

For the verb *vocō*, we see the listing: *vocō, -āre, -āvī, -ātum*. The third principle part is *vocāvī*. Take off the *-ī*, and the perfect stem is *vocāv-*. To this stem we add the perfect personal endings: *-ī, -istī, -it, -imus, -istis, -ērunt*.

    This paradigm is for perfect verbs of the first conjugation.

PERFECT

vocāv*ī*	I called	vocāv*imus*	we called
vocāv*istī*	you called	vocāv*istis*	you (pl.) called
vocāv*it*	he, she, it called	vocāv*ērunt*	they called

This tense may also be conjugated in English as: *I have called, you have called, he has called, we have called, you (pl.) have called, they have called. I did call, you did call, he did call, we did call, you (pl.) did call, they did call.*

The perfect tense for *sum* looks like this:

PERFECT

fu*ī*   I was, I have been   fu*imus*   we have been

fu*istī*   you have been   fu*istis*   you (pl.) have been

fu*it*   he, she, it has been   fu*ērunt*   they have been

The verb *to be* is quite irregular in English. Therefore students need to be taught to think about *fuī* as a perfect verb, even though it seems to have an imperfect meaning (*was*).

The names of the principal parts of a Latin verb are: the present indicative (vocō), the present infinitive (vocāre), the perfect indicative (vocāvī), and the supine or past participle(vocātum).

Lesson Thirteen Exercises

A. Write the noun paradigm for these noun phrases.

toga

[toga]   [togae]

[togae]   [togārum]

[togae]   [togīs]

[togam]   [togās]

[togā]   [togīs]

vir iūcundus

[vir iūcundus]   [virī iūcundī]

[virī iūcundī]   [virōrum iūcundōrum]

[virō iūcundō]   [virīs iūcundīs]

[virum iūcundum]   [virōs iūcundōs]

[virō iūcundō]   [virīs iūcundīs]

magnum templum

[magnum templum]   [magna templa]

[magnī templī]   [magnōrum templōrum]

[magnō templō]   [magnīs templīs]

[magnum templum]   [magna templa]

[magnō templō]   [magnīs templīs]

B. Conjugate these verbs orally in the perfect tense.

arō

cantō

nōminō

pugnō

saltō

> arāvī, arāvistī, arāvit, arāvimus, arāvistis, arāvērunt
>
> cantāvī, cantāvistī, cantāvit, cantāvimus, cantāvistis, cantāvērunt
>
> nōmināvī, nōmināvistī, nōmināvit, nōmināvimus, nōmināvistis, nōmināvērunt
>
> pugnāvī, pugnāvistī, pugnāvit, pugnāvimus, pugnāvistis, pugnāvērunt
>
> saltāvī, saltāvistī, saltāvit, saltāvimus, saltāvistis, saltāvērunt

C. Use each of the verbs in a sentence telling about a single completed past action.

1. arō _____

2. cantō _____

3. nōminō _____

4. pugnō _____

5. saltō _____

D. Study these new vocabulary words.

cūrō, -āre, -āvī, -ātum

dēlectō, -āre, -āvī, -ātum

ōrō, -āre, -āvī, -ātum

capillus, -ī, m

patruus, -ī, m.

adōrō, -āre, -āvī, -ātum	to worship
frūmentum, -ī, n.	grain, corn
herbōsus, -a, -um	grassy
incitō, -āre, -āvī, -ātum	to incite, to urge on
locus, -ī, m.	place (loca, plural neuter)
prātum, -ī, n.	meadow
prōcūl *(adv.)*	far, far away
statim *(adv.)*	at once
subitō *(adv.)*	suddenly
ūnus, -a, -um	one
vehementer *(adv.)*	exceedingly, very much

E. Give ten English derivatives from this lesson's vocabulary.

1. _____   6. _____

2. _____   7. _____

3. _____   8. _____

4. _____   9. _____

5. _____   10. _____

adore, adoration, cure, curator, delectable, incite, oration, capillary, fermentation, location, pratincole, alias, herbacious, unity, union, unison, STAT, vehemently

F. Read the story. Think about the difference in meaning between the imperfect tense and the perfect tense verbs.

Cerēs et Persephonē (A)

Nunc ūnum Deum adōrant et Italī et Britannī. Sed ōlim Rōmānī multōs deōs, multās deās, adōrābant. Dē deīs Rōmānīs fābulās nārrābō. Cerēs erat dea frūmentā; in agrīs frūmentum, in prātīs herbam cūrābat. Flāvum est frūmentum; flāvī erant deae capillī. Caerulea erat deae palla. Persephonē erat fīliā deae. Cerēs fīliam cāram vēhementer amābat. In īnsulā Siciliā Cerēs cum fīlia habitābat. Olim Persephonē in prātīs errābat. Cum puellā aliae puellae errābant, nam locus herbōsus fuit grātus puellīs laetīs. In prātō herbōsō puellae saltābant et cantābant. Multae rosae, multa līlia, in prātīs erant. Līlia alba puellās dēlectābant. Sed Plūtō, patruus puellae, deae fīliam procul spectāvit. Statim puellam vēhementer amāvit. Subitō equōs caeruleōs incitāvit et per prātam properāvit, et puellam perterritam raptāvit. Tum Persephonē,* "O Cerēs," exclāmat, "ubi es? Patruus meus fīliam tuam ad Inferōs portat."

alius, -a, -ud—another

Cerēs, Cereris, f.—Ceres, goddess of grain

Inferī, -ōrum, m. pl.—The Underworld, the realm of the dead

līlium -ī, n.—lily

Persephonē, -ēs, f.—Persephone, daughter of Ceres

Plūtō, -ōnis, m.—Pluto, king of the Underworld

Sicilia, -ae, f.—Sicily

nam (conj.)—for

Now the Italians and the Britons worship one God. But at one time (once) the Romans worshiped many gods and many goddesses. I will tell stories about the Roman gods. Ceres was the goddess of grain; she cared for grain in the fields; she cared for grass in the meadows. Yellow is grain; the hair(s) of the goddess was (were) yellow. Blue was the goddess's cloak. Persephone was the daughter of the goddess. Ceres loved (her) dear daughter very much. On the island Sicily, Ceres lived with (her) daughter. Once Persephone was wandering in the meadows. Other girls were wandering with the girl, for the grassy place was (has been) pleasing to the happy girls. In the grassy meadow the girls danced and sang. Many roses (and) many lilies were in the meadows. White lilies delighted the girls. But Pluto, uncle of the girl, looked at the far away daughter of the goddess. At once he loved the girl very much. Suddenly he urged on (his) blue horses and hurried through the meadow, and seized the frightened girl. Then Persephone exclaimed(cried out), "Oh Ceres, where are you? My uncle carries your daughter to the Underworld."

*The vocative case is used for the noun of address. It is used when speaking directly to a person or persons. It almost always looks like the nominative case (except for masculine nouns ending in *-us*, when the *-us* of the nominative ending changes to *-e.*) The vocative is rarely the first word in a Latin sentence, hence: *Tum Persephonē, "O Cerēs, exclamat, . . . Persephonē exclamat* is separated by the vocative, *Cerēs,* which appears in it's usual second place in the sentence.

G. Answer these questions about the story with complete Latin sentences.

1. Quis (who) erat dea frūmentī?
2. Ubi Cerēs habitābat?
3. Ubi laetae Persephonē et puellae fuērunt?
4. Ubi līlia erant?
5. Cūr (why) Plūtō puellam raptāvit?

---

1. Cerēs dea frūmentī erat.
2. In īnsulā Siciliā Cerēs cum fīliā habitābat.
3. Locus herbōsus fuit grātus puellīs laetīs. (In prātō herbōsō puellae saltābant et cantābant.)
4. Līlia in prātīs erant.
5. Plūtō puellam vehementer amāvit.

Lesson Fourteen

Conjunctions are small words which join together sentences, clauses, phrases, or words. The word *conjunction* comes from two Latin words, *com* (from *cum*, with) and *jungere* (to join).

Here is a list of frequently used Latin conjunctions.

atque—and, and also

aut—or

aut . . . aut—either . . . or

autem—but, however

et—and

et . . . et—both . . . and

itaque—and so

sed—but

quod—because

nam—for

nec—and not, nor

nec . . . nec—neither . . . nor

neque—and not, nor

neque . . . neque—neither . . . nor

An excellent way to learn to use these words well is by writing long sentences using conjunctions!

Lesson Fourteen Exercises

A. Study this new vocabulary.

cibus, -ī, m.

lūna, -ae, f.

īrātus, -a, -um

pōmum, -ī, n.

miser, -era, -erum   unhappy, unfortunate, poor
nusquam *(adv.)*   nowhere
passus, -a, -um   spread out, dishevelled

B. Read the story. Draw a cartoon strip (or three or four pictures in a row) showing what is happening in the story.

Cerēs et Persephonē (B)

Cerēs nōn in Siciliā erat, sed iam ad īnsulam properāvit. Nusquam erat Persephonē. Tum dea, īrāta et perterrita, passīs capillīs per terrās errābat. Per clīvōs altōs, per campōs lātōs, per silvās et agrōs, per terrās et caelum fīliam vocābat. Frustrā agricolās, frustrā lūnam et stellās rōgābat: "Ubi est fīlia mea?" Sed neque agricolae neque lūna neque stellae deae puellam monstrāvērunt. Nōn iam deae miserae grātum erat frūmentum; nōn iam herba erat in prātīs, neque ūvae purpureae in vīneās, neque pōma in agrōs, quod dea īrāta neque herbam neque vīneās neque pōma cūrābat. Frustrā iuvēncī albī agrōs arābant. Nōn iam cibum in plaustrīs magnīs ad oppida portābant.

Ceres was not in Sicily, but now she hurried to the island. Nowhere was Persephone. Then the goddess, angry and frightened, wandered through the earth with hair disheveled. Through high hills and wide plains, through forests and fields, through earth and sky she was calling (her) daughter. In vain she was asking the farmers, in vain (she was asking) the moon and stars, "Where is my daughter?" But neither the farmers nor the moon nor the stars showed the goddess the girl. No longer was grain pleasing to the unhappy goddess; no longer was grass in the meadows, nor purple grapes in the vineyards, nor fruit in the fields, because the angry goddess cared for neither the grass nor the vineyards, nor the fruit. In vain the white bullocks were plowing the fields. No longer were they carrying food in great wagons to the towns.

Lesson Fifteen

The *pluperfect tense* is sometimes called the past perfect tense. *Pluperfect* comes from two Latin words *plus* and *perfect*, and it means "more than perfect." A pluperfect action was completed before another past action. We use the helping verb *had* with this tense.

Before his death, Joshua had commanded *the Israelites well.*

But the people had not destroyed *their enemies before they stopped to rest.*

God had made *their lives hard so they would remember Him.*

When they had prayed *for help, God sent them judges.*

Barak had been afraid *to go into battle before Deborah, the woman judge, agreed to go with him.*

On a timeline, the pluperfect would look like this:

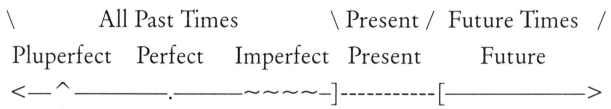

To form a pluperfect tense verb in Latin, we find the verb's perfect stem (the third principal part). Then we add the tense sign (*erā*) and the personal endings (*-m, -s, -t, -mus, -tis, -nt*).

Pluperfect tense = perfect stem + *erā* + personal endings

This is the paradigm for pluperfect, first conjugation verbs.

PLUPERFECT

vocā*veram*	I had called	vocā*verāmus*	we had called
vocā*verās*	you had called	vocā*verātis*	you (pl.) had called
vocā*verat*	he, she, it had called	vocā*verant*	they had called

The pluperfect paradigm for *sum* looks like this:

PLUPERFECT

fu*eram*	I had been	fu*erāmus*	we had been
fu*erās*	you had been	fu*erātis*	you (pl.) had been
fu*erat*	he, she, it had been	fu*erant*	they had been

Lesson Fifteen Excercises

A. Tell (or write) the tense of the verbs in these English sentences. Choose from present(P), imperfect(I), future(F), perfect(PF), and pluperfect(PP).

_____1. Esau was the favored son of his father, Isaac.

_____ 2. Rebekah had made Jacob her favorite.

_____ 3. Perhaps Esau's choice of Canaanite wives made Rebekah grieved (*adj.*) with him.

_____ 4. Esau did not care that God had cursed the Canaanites.

_____ 5. Still Isaac loves his wayward son.

_____ 6. Isaac was planning to give Esau the blessing of the firstborn.

_____ 7. But Rebekah planned with Jacob to trick Isaac.

_____ 8. Jacob killed two goats which his mother fixed to taste like venison.

_____ 9. After Isaac had blessed Jacob, Esau appeared with his meal for his father.

_____ 10. Esau was searching for Jacob, but Jacob had gone to his Uncle's land.

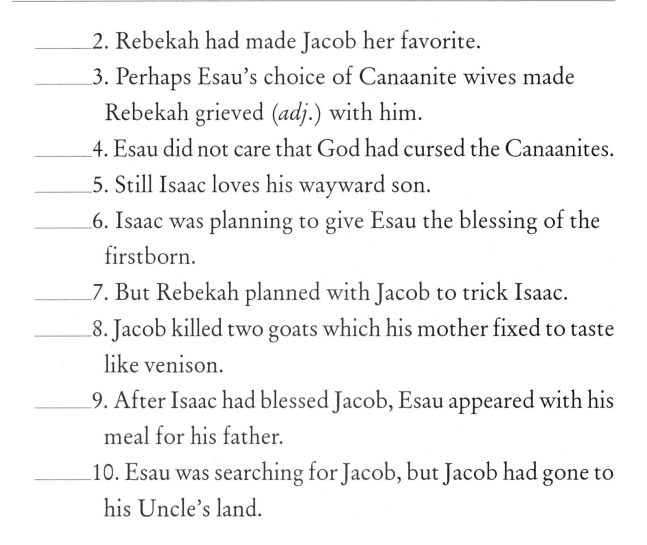

I   1. Esau <u>was</u> the favored son of his father, Isaac.
PP   2. Rebekah <u>had made</u> Jacob her favorite.
PF   3. Perhaps Esau's choice of Canaanite wives <u>made</u> Rebekah grieved (*adj.*) with him.
PF/PP   4. Esau <u>did not care</u> that God <u>had cursed</u> the Canaanites.
P   5. Still Isaac <u>loves</u> his wayward son.
I   6. Isaac <u>was planning</u> to give Esau the blessing of the firstborn.
PF   7. But Rebekah <u>planned</u> with Jacob to trick Isaac.
PF/PF   8. Jacob <u>killed</u> two goats which his mother <u>fixed</u> to taste like venison.
PP/PF   9. After Isaac <u>had blessed</u> Jacob, Esau <u>appeared</u> with his meal for his father.
I/PP   10. Esau <u>was searching</u> for Jacob, but Jacob <u>had gone</u> to his Uncle's land.

B. Study this new vocabulary.

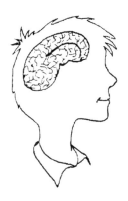

animus, -ī, m.

auxilium, auxiliī, n.

ēvolō, -āre, -āvī -ātum

familia, -ae, f.

populus, -ī, m.

ventus, -ī, m.

apportō, -āre, -āvī, -ātum	to bring, to take
celeriter *(adv.)*	quickly
dictum, -ī, n	a saying
factum, -ī, n.	deed, act
intereā *(adv.)*	meanwhile
lectus, -ī, m.	bed, couch
māne *(adv.)*	in the morning
memoria, -ae, f.	memory
mox *(adv.)*	soon
propter *(prep. w/ acc.)*	on account of, because of
semper *(adv.)*	always

C. Conjugate *apportō* and *ēvolō* in the perfect and pluperfect tenses. Conjugate *sum* in all five tenses.

PERFECT

apportāvī	[apportāvimus]
[apportāvistī]	[apportāvistis]
[apportāvit]	[apportāvērunt]

PLUPERFECT

[apportāverām]	[apportāverāmus]
[apportāverās]	[apportāverātis]
[apportāverat]	[apportāverant]

PERFECT

ēvolāvī	[ēvolāvimus]
[ēvolāvistī]	[ēvolāvistis]
[ēvolāvit]	[ēvolāvērunt]

PLUPERFECT

[ēvolāveram]	[ēvolāverāmus]
[ēvolāverās]	[ēvolāverātis]
[ēvolāverat]	[ēvolāverant]

PRESENT

sum	[sumus]
[es]	[estis]
[est]	[sunt]

IMPERFECT

[eram]	[erāmus]
[erās]	[erātis]
[erat]	[erant]

FUTURE

[erō]	[erimus]
[eris]	[eritis]
[erit]	[erunt]

PERFECT

[fuī] _____	[fuimus] _____
[fuistī] _____	[fuistis] _____
[fuit] _____	[fuērunt] _____

PLUPERFECT

[fueram] _____	[fuerāmus] _____
[fuerās] _____	[fuerātis] _____
[fuerat] _____	[fuerant] _____

D. Read the story of Jacob and Esau in Genesis 27. Next read this short version of the story. Notice the use of different tenses. Then draw a picture on the next page to show your understanding of the part of the story written here.

Isaac·oculīs nōn spectāverat, vocāvitque Esau fīlium suum maiorem et "Filī mī," inquit. Esau respondit, "Adsum."

"Tibi ōrō, bēstiam armīs tuīs necā et mihi cēnam creā," dixit Isaac. Ita Esau in silvā et in agrīs ambulābat.

Intereā Rebekah fīliō suō Jacob narrāverat, "Necā duās parvās bēstiās, dabimus cibum Isaac." Tum Rebekah togam Esau portāverat et Jacob togam cum multīs capillīs creāverat. Posteā Jacob ad Isaac cibum portāvit. Isaac putāvit Jacob Esau esse. Tum Isaac Jacob magnum benedictum dedit.

Mox Esau cibum suum portāvit ad Isaac. "Nōn es Esau," dixit Isaac, "Māne Esau erat hic. Esau benedictum dedī." Lacrimīs sed frustrā, Esau ōrāvit, "Dā mihi benedictum." Tum Isaac Esau parvum benedictum dedit. Nunc Esau īrātus erat propter Jacob. Familia maesta erat quod Jacob et Rebekah stultī et scelerātī fuerant.

maiorem—older

fīlī mī—my son

adsum, adesse, adfuī—to be present

tibi—to you

creō, -āre, -āvī, -ātum—create, make

necā—Kill! a command

putō, -āre, -āvī, -ātum—to think

posteā—afterwards

dixit—he said

hic (adv.)—here

dā—Give!

stultus, -a, -um—foolish

scelerātus, -a, -um—wicked

Isaac did not see with his eyes, and he called Esau his older son and said, "My Son." Esau responded, "I am here."

"I beg you, kill a beast with your weapons and make me a dinner," said Isaac. So Esau walked in the forests and in the fields.

Meanwhile Rebekah told her son Jacob, "Kill two small beasts, and we will make food for Isaac." Then Rebekah had carried Esau's toga and made Jacob a toga with many hairs. Afterwards Jacob carried food to Isaac. Isaac thought Jacob to be Esau. Then Isaac gave Jacob a great blessing.

Soon Esau carried his food to Isaac. "You are not Esau," said Isaac, "this morning Esau was here. I have given Esau his blessing." With tears, but in vain, Esau begged, "Give me a blessing." Then Isaac gave Esau a small blessing. Now Esau was angry because of Jacob. The household was sad because Jacob and Rebekah had been foolish and wicked.

Lesson Sixteen

The last verb tense we have to learn is the *future perfect* tense. This tense is hardly ever seen in English; it's meaning is understood, not directly stated. In Latin, also, this tense does not often appear, but learning it will complete our ability to conjugate a verb and prepare us for those times it is used.

The future perfect tense tells one future action which happens before another future action. (The second future action will be in the future tense.) The helping verbs for this tense are *will have*.

Here are some examples of future perfect tense verbs in English sentences.

When you will have plowed *the field, we will plant it.*

Before he will have jumped *his final hurdle he* will have run *ten miles.*

After he will have finished *his ice cream, he will go to bed.*

On a timeline, the future perfect would look like this:

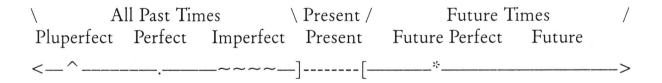

To form a future perfect tense verb in Latin, we find the verb's perfect stem (the third principal part). Then we add the tense sign (*eri*) and the personal endings (*-ō, -s, -t, -mus, -tis, -nt*).

Future Perfect tense = perfect stem + *eri* + personal endings.

This is the paradigm for future perfect, first conjugation verbs:

FUTURE PERFECT

vocāver*ō*	I will have called	vocāver*imus*	we will have called
vocāver*is*	you will have called	vocāver*itis*	you (pl.) will have called
vocāver*it*	he, she, it will have called	vocāver*int*	they will have called

The future perfect paradigm for *sum* looks like this:

FUTURE PERFECT

fuer*ō*	I will have been	fuer*imus*	we will have been
fuer*is*	you will have been	fuer*itis*	you (pl.) will have been
fuer*it*	he, she, it will have been	fuer*int*	they will have been

Lesson Sixteen Exercises

A. Study these vocabulary words.

aeger, aegra, aegrum

gelidus, -a, -um

osculum, -ī, n.

saxum, -ī, n.

adhūc *(adv.)*	still, yet
cūnae, -ārum, f.	cradle
diū *(adv.)*	for a long time
dīvīnus, -a, -um	divine
ē, ex *(prep. w/ abl.)*	out of, from
ecce	behold
gremium, -ī, n.	lap
ibi *(adv.)*	there
ignōtus, -a, -um	unknown
maestus, -a, -um	sad
mīrus, -a, -um	wonderful
plēnus, -a, -um	full
post *(prep. w/ acc.)*	after
rusticus, -a, -um	rustic, belonging to the country
tamen *(adv.)*	however, still, nevertheless
tandem *(adv.)*	at last
tōtus, -a, -um	whole

B. Use each of this lesson's adjectives in a Latin sentence with a future perfect verb.

1. aeger   _____

2. dīvīnus   _____

3. gelidus   _____

4. ignōtus   _____

5. maestus   _____

6. mīrus   _____

7. plēnus   _____

8. rusticus   _____

9. tōtus   _____

10. purpureus   _____

C. Tell why?

1. Why does the word for cradle only have plural forms?

2. Why is an *osculation* not something proper to do in public? (or at least not usually!)

3. Why does a plant family have the name *saxifrage*?

4. Why is an *exit* a place for going out?

5. Why is a feeling of *plenitude* a good thing?

---

1. A cradle has *two* runners.
2. Usually we don't *kiss* in public.
3. These plants break *rocks*.
4. *Ex* means *out of.*
5. A *full* feeling is usually quite satisfying!

DAILY ORAL REVIEW

Conjugate a different verb each day. Use all six tenses.

Decline an adjective/noun phrase each day.

Review the definitions of the parts of speech.

Lesson Seventeen

A way to look quickly at all the tenses of a verb is called a *synopsis*. To do a synopsis of any verb, we simply follow the same personal pronoun through all the tenses. In English we would do a synopsis of *talk* in the first person, singular, by saying: *I talk, I was talking, I shall talk, I have talked, I had talked, I shall have talked.* To keep from being confused, we always use the same order for a conjugation or a synopsis. We follow the order in which we learned the tenses: present, imperfect, future, perfect, pluperfect, future perfect.

A synopsis of *vocō* in the third person, singular looks like this:

PRESENT	voca*t*
IMPERFECT	vocā*bat*
FUTURE	vocā*bit*
PERFECT	vocā*vit*
PLUPERFECT	vocā*verat*
FUTURE PERFECT	vocā*verit*

Lesson Seventeen Exercises

A. Do a synopsis of these verbs as required.

CANTŌ: FIRST PERSON, SINGULAR

Present	[cantō]	
Imperfect	[cantābam]	
Future	[cantābō]	
Perfect	[cantāvī]	
PluPerfect	[cantāveram]	
Future Perfect	[cantāverō]	

ARŌ: SECOND PERSON, PLURAL

[arātis] _____

[arābātis] _____

[arābitis] _____

[arāvistis] _____

[arāverātis] _____

[arāveritis] _____

EXCLĀMŌ: FIRST PERSON, PLURAL

[exclāmāmus] _____

[exclāmābāmus] _____

[exclāmābimus] _____

[exclāmāvimus] _____

[exclāmāverāmus] _____

[exclāmāverimus] _____

Lesson Eighteen

There are four family groups, or conjugations, of Latin verbs. The first conjugation has an infinitive ending in *-āre*. The second group has an infinitive ending in *-ēre*. Many of the tenses will look almost like first conjugation tenses, but they will have an *-ē-* in the present stem. These verbs will be listed in a vocabulary or dictionary listing as: *sedeō, -ēre, sēdī, sessum*. Each verb will have its very own third and fourth principal part. They are not as easy to remember as the *-āre, -āvī, -ātum* pattern of first conjugation. It is important to memorize all four parts when you first learn the vocabulary.

The second conjugation paradigm for the present tense looks like this:

PRESENT

teneō	I hold, I am holding, I do hold	tenēmus	we hold
tenēs	you hold	tenētis	you (pl.) hold
tenet	he, she, it holds	tenent	they hold

The macrons follow the same pattern as they did in the first conjugation. If the students are learning the macrons, show them the shallow slipper that is formed by drawing a line around the first and second plural and extending it to include the second person singular as the toe of the slipper.

The second conjugation paradigm for the imperfect tense looks like this:

IMPERFECT

tenē*bam*	I was holding	tenē*bāmus*	we were holding
tenē*bās*	you were holding	tenē*bātis*	you (pl.) were holding
tenē*bat*	he, she, it was holding	tenē*bant*	they were holding

The second conjugation paradigm for the future tense looks like this:

FUTURE

tenē*bō*	I shall hold	tenē*bimus*	we shall hold
tenē*bis*	you will hold	tenē*bitis*	you (pl.) will hold
tenē*bit*	he, she, it will hold	tenē*bunt*	they will hold

Lesson Eighteen Exercises

A. Study these new vocabulary words.

habeō, habēre, habuī, habitum   iactō, iactāre, iactāvī, iactum

doceō, docēre, docuī, doctum	to teach
fleō, flēre, flēvī, flētum	to weep, to cry
flōreō, flōrēre, flōruī, — — —	to flourish, to flower
fulgeō, fulgēre, fulsī, — — —	to shine
iaceo, -ere, -cui, -citum	to lie
maneō, manēre, mānsī, mansum	to stay, to remain
sedeō, sedēre, sēdī, sessum	to sit
teneō, tenēre, tenuī, tentum	to hold
timeō, timēre, timuī, — — —	to fear, to be afraid
valeō, valēre, valuī, — — —	to be well
videō, vidēre, vīdī, vīsum	to see

B. Orally conjugate *habeō*, *sedeō*, and *video* in the present, imperfect, and future tenses.

habeō, habēs, habet, habēmus, habētis, habent; habēbam, habēbās, habēbat, habēbāmus, habēbātis, habēbant; habēbō, habēbis, habēbit, habēbimus, habēbitis, habēbunt

sedeō, sedēs, sedet, sedēmus, sedētis, sedent; sedēbam, sedēbās, sedēbat, sedēbāmus, sedēbātis, sedēbant; sedēbō, sedēbis, sedēbit, sedēbimus, sedēbitis, sedēbunt

videō, vidēs, videt, vidēmus, vidētis, vident; vidēbam, vidēbās, vidēbat, vidēbāmus, vidēbātis, vidēbant; vidēbō, vidēbis, vidēbit, vidēbimus, vidēbitis, vidēbunt

C. Make a list of at least ten English words which come from this lesson's vocabulary. Use a stilum nigrum.

habit, habitude, habitus, eject, remain, mansion, sedan, sedate, sedentary, sedilia, sediment, docent, docile, fulgent, fulgurous, timid, timorous, florid, florish

D. Read the story. Circle each verb stilō flavō.

CERĒS ET PERSEPHONĒ (C)

Tandem Cerēs prope parvam casam agricolae in saxō gelidō sedēbat. Dea maesta diū lacrimābat. Tum ē casā parva puella ad deam vēnit. Puellae oculī plenī erant lacrimārum. "Parvum puerum," inquit, "habēmus. In cūnīs aeger iacet. Lacrimāmus, quod aeger est puer." Tum Cerēs lacrimās suās tenuit, et cum puellā ad casam properāvit.

Ibi Metanīra fīlium aegrum in gremiō tenēbat. Fīlius Metanīrae Triptolemus erat. Lacrimābant et agricola et Metanīra et parva puella, quod nōn valēbat puer. Tum Cerēs puerō osculum dedit, et ecce! statim valuit puer. Mīrum et dīvīnum erat osculum deae. Laetae erant et agricola et Metanīra et puella. Iam laetus et validus puer in cūnīs dormītābat. Tum Cerēs Triptolemum in gremiō suō tenuit. Dea cum tōtā familiā cēnam habuit; in mensā erant ūvae purpureae et pōma iūcunda. Adhūc ignōta erant Italīs Graecīsque et vīnum et frūmentum. Deae tamen flāvae grāta erat cēna rustica. Post cēnam in casā agricolae dea manēbat et cotidiē Triptolemum cūrābat.

Tandem Cerēs prope parvam agricolae casam in saxō gelidō sedēbat. Dea maesta diū lacrimābat. Tum ē casā puella parva ad deam vēnit. Puellae oculī plenī erant lacrimārum. "Puerum parvum," inquit, "habēmus. In cūnīs aeger iacet. Lacrimāmus, quod aeger est puer." Tum Cerēs lacrimās suās tenuit, et cum puellā ad casam properāvit.

Ibi Metanīra fīlium aegrum in gremiō tenēbat. Fīlius Metanīrae Triptolemus erat. Lacrimābant et agricola et Metanīra et puella parva, quod nōn valēbat puer. Tum Cerēs puerō osculum dedit, et ecce! statim valuit puer. Mīrum et dīvīnum est osculum deae. Laetā erant et agricola et Metanīra et puella. Iam laetus et validus puer in cūnīs dormītābat. Tum Cerēs Triptolemum in gremiō suō tenuit. Dea cum tōtā familiā cēnam habuit; in mensā erant ūvae purpureae et pōma iūcunda. Adhūc ignōta erant Italīs Graecīsque et vīnum et frūmentum. Deae tamen flāvae grāta erat rustica cēna. Post cēnam in agricolae casā dea manēbat et cotidiē Triptolemum cūrābat.

At last Ceres sat on a cold rock near a farmer's small cottage. The unhappy goddess cried for a long time. Then a small girl came from the cottage to the goddess. The girl's eyes were full of tears. "We have a small boy," she said. "He lies sick in (his) cradle. We are weeping because the boy is sick." Then Ceres held (back) her own tears and hurried to the cottage with the girl.

There Metanira was holding (her) sick son on her lap. The son of Metanira was Triptolemus. They were crying, the farmer and Metanira and the small girl, because the boy was not well. Then Ceres gave the boy a kiss, and behold! instantly (at once) the boy was well. Wonderful and divine was the kiss of the goddess. They were happy, both the farmer and Metanira and the girl. Now the strong and happy boy slept in (his) cradle. Then Ceres held Triptolemus on her lap. The goddess had food with the whole family; on the table were purple grapes and pleasant fruit. Still unknown to the Italians and the Greeks were both wine and grain. To the yellow-haired goddess, however, the country supper was pleasing. After supper the goddess stayed in the farmer's cottage and cared for Triptolemus every day.

Teacher's Note: Some of these verbs are second conjugation, perfect tense. We will learn this form in the next lesson. Astute students will notice this and will identify the form because they have had this vocabulary and the perfect tense follows the same rules in first and second conjugation. For students who are troubled by the new form, a brief preview of lesson nineteen may be desired.

Lesson Nineteen

In Latin the perfect tense for the second conjugation is formed by finding the perfect stem of the verb and adding the perfect tense personal endings. This is a special set of endings used only for this tense. To find the perfect stem, think of the third principal part of the verb and take off the -ī.

Perfect stem = third principal part -ī

Perfect tense =
perfect stem + perfect personal endings

For the verb *teneō*, we see the listing: *teneō, tenēre, tenuī, tentum.* The third principle part is *tenuī.* Take off the -ī, and the perfect stem is *tenu-.* To this stem we add the perfect personal endings: *-ī, -istī, -it, -imus, -istis, -ērunt.*

This is the paradigm for second conjugation perfect verbs.

Perfect

tenu*ī*	I held, I have held	tenu*imus*	we held
tenu*istī*	you held	tenu*istis*	you (pl.) held
tenu*it*	he, she, it held	tenu*ērunt*	they held

The pluperfect and future perfect tenses follow the same rules as for first conjugation verbs.

This is the paradigm for pluperfect verbs of the second conjugation.

PluPerfect tense =
perfect stem + *erā* + personal endings

PluPerfect

tenu*eram*	I had held	tenu*erāmus*	we had held
tenu*erās*	you had held	tenu*erātis*	you (pl.) had held
tenu*erat*	he, she, it had held	tenu*erant*	they had held

Future Perfect tense = perfect stem + *eri* + personal endings

---

This is the paradigm for future perfect verbs of the second conjugation.

FUTURE PERFECT

tenu*erō*	I will have held	tenu*erimus*	we will have held
tenu*eris*	you will have held	tenu*eritis*	you (pl.) will have held
tenu*erit*	he, she, it will have held	tenu*erint*	they will have held

Lesson Nineteen Exercises

A. Review vocabulary from lessons 10–18.

B. Orally conjugate *portō* and *sedeō* in all six tenses.

---

portō, portās, portat, portāmus, portātis, portant; portābam, portābās, portābat, portābāmus, portābātis, portābant; portābō, portābis, portābit, portābimus, portābitis, portābunt; portāvī, portāvistī, portāvit, portāvimus, portāvistis, portāvērunt; portāveram, portāverās, portāverat, portāverāmus, portāverātis, portāverant; portāverō, portāveris, portāverit, portāverimus, portāveritis, portāverint

sedeō, sedēs, sedet, sedēmus, sedētis, sedent; sedēbam, sedēbās, sedēbat, sedēbāmus, sedēbātis, sedēbant; sedēbō, sedēbis, sedēbit, sedēbimus, sedēbitis, sedēbunt; sēdī, sēdistī, sēdit, sēdimus, sēdistis, sēdērunt; sēderam, sēderās, sēderat, sēderāmus, sēderātis, sēderant; sēderō, sēderis, sēderit, sēderimus, sēderitis, sēderint

C. Do a complete synopsis (all six tenses) of *maneō*, *iaceō*, and *doceō* in the third person plural.

MANEŌ:

Present	[manent]
Imperfect	[manēbant]
Future	[manēbunt]
Perfect	[mānsērunt]
PluPerfect	[mānserant]
Future Perfect	[mānserint]

IACEŌ:

[iacent]

[iacēbant]

[iacēbunt]

[iacuērunt]

[iacuerant]

[iacuerint]

DOCEŌ:

[docent]

[docēbant]

[docēbunt]

[docuērunt]

[docuerant]

[docuerint]

D. How would you say this in Latin?

1. First, the temple had held the altars, then it held many rocks.

2. Before I sleep, I will pray and praise God. (In Latin it will look like: Before I will sleep, I will have prayed and I will have praised God.)

3. They were building cottages, but she wanted one wide palace.

4. The forest and the red earth were beautiful on every side.

5. The wicked woman's kind husband was sound asleep. (was lying in a deep sleep.)

> 1. Primō templum arās habuerat, deinde multa saxa habuit.
> 2. Ante dormītābō, orāverō et Deum laudāverō.
> 3. Casās aedificābant, sed unam rēgiam lātam dēsīderāvit.
> 4. Silva et terra rubra undique pulchrae erant.
> 5. Vir benignus fēminae scelerātae in somnō altō iacēbat.
> NOTE: There may be other correct renderings.

E. Read the story.

Iam lūna et stellae in caelō fulgēbant. Umbrae terrās et pontum profundum cēlābant. Per terrās virī et fēminae animōs somnō laxābant. Sed somnus Metanīram nōn tenēbat; furtim deam cum puerō spectābat.

Cerēs prope puerī cūnās stābat. Vērba mīra et dīvīna cantābat. Tum puerum in gremiō tenuit, et ad focum ambulāvit. Ecce! Triptolemus in focō inter flammās iacēbat sed laetus erat puer; neque focum neque flammās timuit. Sed Metanīra, perterrita, "O fīlī mī," exclāmāvit, et ad focum properāvit.

Tum dea īrāta puerum ē flammās raptāvit et humī iactāvit, et Metanīrae, "O fēmina," inquit, " stulta et scelerāta fuistī. Nōn deus erit Triptolemus, quod stultae fēminae est fīlius. Sed in gremiō deae iacuit; itaque magnus vir erit. Et ego et Persephonē, fīlia mea, Triptolemum docēbimus et cūrābimus. Agricolārum magister erit, nam frūmentum et vīnum agricolīs monstrābit."

---

axō, -āre, -āvī, -ātum—to relax, to loosen　　*pontus, -ī, m.*—sea
focus, -ī, m.—hearth　　*somnus, -ī m.*—sleep
furtim (adv.)—secretly, stealthily　　*verbum, -ī, n.*—word

Now the moon and stars were shining in the sky. Shadows were hiding the lands and the deep sea. Through the lands men and women relaxed (their) minds by sleep. But sleep did not hold Metanira; secretly she was watching the goddess with the boy.

Ceres was standing near the boy's cradle. She was singing wonderful and divine words. Then she held the boy on (her) lap, and walked to the hearth. Behold! Triptolemus was lying in the hearth among the flames, but the boy was happy; he feared neither the hearth nor the flames. But frightened Metanira shouted out (exclaimed), "Oh, my son!" and hurried to the hearth.

Then the angry goddess seized (grabbed) the boy from the flames and tossed him (the boy) on the ground and said to Metanira, "Oh woman, you have been foolish and wicked. Triptolemus will not be a god, because he is the son of a wicked and foolish woman. But he laid in the lap of a goddess; therefore he will be a great man. Both I and Persephone, my daughter, will teach Triptolemus and (we will) care for him. He will be a teacher of the farmers, for he will show grain and wine to the farmers.

F. Answer these questions about the grammatical constructions in the story.

1. What case is used for *pontum profundum*? Why?

2. What case is used for *virī* (*virī et fēminae*)? Why?

3. What case is used for *somnō*? Why?

4. What case is used for *focum* (*ad focum*)? Why?

5. Look at the sentence: *Verba mīra et dīvīna cantābat.* Why is the verb singular?

6. Make up your own question. Can you think of one your classmates can't answer?

---

1. accusative; direct object
2. nominative; subject
3. ablative; ablative of means—tells by what means they relaxed their minds
4. accusative; after preposition *ad*
5. goddess is the subject, not *verba* as may be thought at first glance

Optional Unit—Stories

Tum Cerēs ē casā agricolae ambulāvit. Sed flēvērunt familia et flēvit Triptolemus, quod nōn iam in gremiō deae dormītābat. Māne agricola virōs et fēminās locī convocāvit, et dicta deae et facta narrāvit. Deinde virī et fēminae multa saxa apportāvērunt et magnum templum aedificāvērunt. In templī ārīs victimās mactāvērunt, et deam adōrāvērunt. Grāta erant deae dōna populī, et Cerēs templum diū habitābat. Intereā in ārīs aliōrum deōrum neque pōma neque ūvae neque rosae iacēbant. Nōn iam herba in prātīs, nōn iam pōma in agrīs flōrēbant, quod adhūc Cerēs propter fīliam flēbat. Itaque Iuppiter deae, "Plūto," inquit, "fīliam tuam habet. Persephonē rēgīna Inferōrum est. Sed Mecurius ad regnum Inferōrum properābit, et puellam ad templum tuum celeriter apportābit." Deinde Mercurius ad Inferōs properāvit. Persephonē cum virō suō in lectō sedēbat. Misera erat puella, quod adhūc deam cāram dēsīderābat. Sed Mercurium vidēbat et laeta fuit. "Iterum," inquit, "deam cāram vidēbo, iterum Cerēs fīliam suam habēbit." Tum Plūto verbīs benignīs puellam ōrāvit : "O Persephonē, memoriae tuae grātus semper erit Plūto; iterum rēgīna Inferōrum eris. Nunc caeruleum est caelum, iūcunda sunt prāta, sed mox gelidum erit caelum, gelidī erunt et ventī et agrī. Tum iterum virum tuum et regnum Inferōrum dēsīderābis. Valē, O cāra rēgīna." Tum Persephonē cum Mercuriō ē regnō Inferōrum properāvit. Mercurius equōs validōs incitāvit, et equī per clīvōs altōs, per campōs lātōs libenter properāvērunt. Tandem Persephonē templum deae flāvae vidēbat. Puella laeta verbīs laetīs deam vocāvit. Cerēs magnō gaudiō ē templō ēvolāvit, et fīliae cārae multa oscula dabat. Subitō per terrās herba in prātīs, ūvae in vīneīs undique flōrēbant, quod nōn iam flēbant Cerēs et Persephonē. Cēterī quoque deī laetī erant, quod agricolae ad templa multa dōna apportābant et in ārīs victimās mactābant.

Then Ceres walked from the cottage of the farmer. But the family wept and Triptolemus wept because he no longer was sleeping in the goddess's lap. In the morning the farmer called the men and women to the place and told the sayings and deeds of the goddess. Then the men and women brought many rocks and built a large temple. On the altars of the temple they offered up victims and worshipped the goddess. Pleasing to the goddess were the gifts of the people and Ceres was living in the temple for a long time. Meanwhile on the altars of the other gods neither fruit, nor grapes, nor roses were lying. No longer grass in the meadows, no longer fruit in the fields flourished, because still Ceres was weeping because of (her) daughter. Therefore Jupiter said to the goddess, "Pluto has your daughter. Persephone is queen of the Underworld. But Mercury will hurry to the kingdom of the Underworld and will quickly bring the girl to your temple. Then Mercury hurried to the Underworld. Persephone was sitting with her man in bed. The girl was unhappy, because still she missed the dear goddess. But she saw Mercury and she was happy. "Again," she said, "I will see (my) dear goddess, again Ceres will have her daughter." Then Pluto begged the girl with kind words, "Oh, Persephone, Pluto always will be pleasing to your memory; again you will be queen of the Underworld. Now blue is the sky, pleasant are the meadows, but soon cold will be the sky, both the winds and the fields will be cold. Then again you will miss your man and the kingdom of the Underworld. Be well (good-bye), oh, dear queen." Then Persephone hurried with Mercury from the kingdom of the Underworld. Mercury urged on the strong horses, and the horses across (through) high hills and wide plains willingly hurried. Finally Persephone saw (was seeing) the temple of the yellow-haired goddess. The happy girl called the goddess with glad words. Ceres flew from the temple with great joy, and gave (was giving) (her) dear daughter many kisses. Suddenly through the lands grasses in meadows, grapes on vines flourished everywhere, because no longer were crying Ceres and Persephone. The rest of the gods also were happy, because the farmers were carrying to the (their) temples many gifts and they were sacrificing many victims on the altars.

deinde (adv.)—then, next

Iuppiter, Iovis, m.—Jupiter, king of the gods

Mercurius, -ī, m.—Mercury, messenger of the gods

gaudium, -ī, n.—joy

regnum, -ī, n.—kingdom

valē, valēte (pl.)—goodbye (be well)

cēterī, -ae, -a—the rest

libenter (adv.)—willingly, gladly

Lesson Twenty

We learned that there are five declensions for Latin nouns. In this text we will learn the third declension, which is a large noun family. The fourth and fifth declensions we will study in a later text.

The third declension has nouns that are masculine, feminine, or neuter in gender. All third declension nouns have a genitive form

---

First declension genitive ends in *-ae*.
Second declension genitive ends in *-ī*
Third declension genitive ends in *-is*.

---

ending in *-is*. The good habits we've begun by learning the gender with the vocabulary word will be even more useful now. It is also important in this declension to memorize each genitive form so that we have the correct stem on which to add the case endings.

Masculine and feminine nouns of the third declension have the same paradigm. The neuter paradigm is a bit different because it follows the neuter noun rule. (The nominative and accusative cases look alike, and the nominative and accusative plurals end in *-a*.)

This is the paradigm for *masculine* and *feminine* third declension nouns.

CASE	SINGULAR	PLURAL
Nominative	mīles	mīlitēs
Genitive	mīlitis	mīlitum
Dative	mīlitī	mīlitibus
Accusative	mīlitem	mīlitēs
Ablative	mīlite	mīlitibus

This is the paradigm for *neuter* third declension nouns.

CASE	SINGULAR	PLURAL
Nominative	caput	capita
Genitive	capitis	capitum
Dative	capitī	capitibus
Accusative	caput	capita
Ablative	capite	capitibus

Most of the words for members of the family (father, mother, aunt, uncle, brother, sister, etc.) come from third declension nouns. Many words for parts of the body and the words for plants and animals also come from third declension nouns.

Here are some hints for remembering the genitive and the gender of third declension nouns:

Nouns of one syllable ending in -*x* are mostly feminine.

Nouns of one syllable ending in *consonant* + -*s* are feminine. (except *fōns, mōns, pōns,* and *dēns,* which are masculine)

English derivatives sometimes give clues about the genitive form: *dent*al (dēns, *dent*is, m. tooth) *leg*al (lēx, *lēg*is, f. law).

The exercises for this lesson will contain many new vocabulary words from these three groups. Study each group of words until you are comfortable with it. Then move on to the next exercise.

Lesson Twenty Exercises

A. Study the vocabulary for family members. Notice that not all the words are from the third declension.

FAMILY TREE

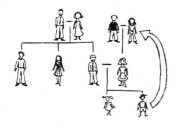

avia, -ae, f. – grandmother

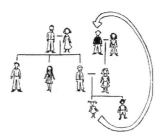

avus, -ī, m. – grandfather

pater, patris, m. – father

māter, matris, f.– mother

frāter, frātris, m. – brother

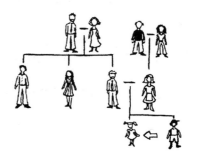

soror, sorōris, f. – sister

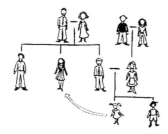

amita, -ae, f. – aunt

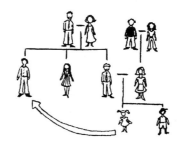

patruus, -ī, m. – uncle

nepos, nepōtis, m. – grandson

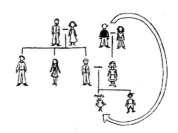

neptis, neptis*, f. – granddaughter

uxor, -ōris, f. – wife

*I-stem noun, Lesson 21

līberī, -ōrum, m. pl.	children
sōbrīna, -ae, f.	cousin (only on the mother's side)
sōbrīnus -ī, m.	cousin
	[To speak of a cousin on the father's side, one must use the third declension adjective (in a future lesson!) patruēlis, -e]
virgō, -inis, f.	virgin, young woman

B. Practice the third declension masculine/feminine paradigm using pater, māter, frāter, soror. Then write the paradigms for *pater bonus* and *māter bona*! Remember: an adjective agrees with the noun it modifies in gender, number, and case.

pater bonus

[patris bonī]

[patrī bonī]

[patrem bonum]

[patre bonō]

[patrēs bonī]

[patrum bonōrum]

[patribus bonīs]

[patrēs bonōs]

[patribus bonīs]

māter bona

[mātris bonae]

[mātrī bonae]

[mātrem bonam]

[mātre bonā]

[mātrēs bonae]

[matrum bonārum]

[mātribus bonīs]

[mātrēs bonās]

[mātribus bonīs]

Encourage student to be diligent in thinking of the paradigm case by case, rather than writing all the stems, then going back and adding the case endings. This latter method may seem quicker or easier for test purposes, but it will detract from the student's speed in reading and writing Latin sentences.

C. From the vocabulary in this lesson, tell how we may have derived these English words and phrases.

Fraternal Order of Police

maternal instincts

paternalistic

nepotism

sorority

virgin

uxorious

D. Write a Latin composition about your family. Be sure to use descriptive adjectives for each person.

E. Study the parts of the body. Take turns with your classmates inventing sentences for a story about a very sick man. Be sure to have your adjectives agreeing with the nouns they modify in gender, number, and case.

caput, capitis, n. – head

cor, cordis, n. – heart

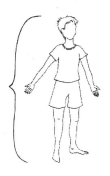

corpus, corporis, n. – body

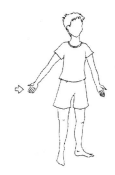

dextra, -ae, f. – right hand

bracchium, -ī, n. – arm

collum, -ī, n. – neck

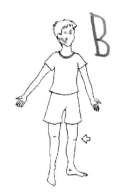

genu, -ūs, n. (IV declension) – knee

pectus, -oris, n. – breast

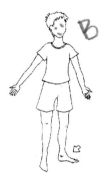

pēs, pedis*, m. – foot

sinistra, -ae, f. – left hand

sinistrum, -ī, n. – left side

oculus, oculī, m. – eye

*I-stem noun, Lesson 21

Lesson Twenty-One

The third declension has a set of nouns which are called *I-stem* nouns. The paradigm for masculine and feminine I-stems differs from the regular third declension only in the genitive plural which ends in *-ium*. The neuter paradigm differs in four places (ablative singular, nominative and accusative plural, genitive plural).

To remember which third declension nouns are I-stems, follow these rules.

M/F I-stems:
1) nominative ends in *-es or -is* <u>and</u> genitive
   has same number of syllables as nominative
2) nominative singular ends in *-ns* or *-rs*
3) nominative singular is one syllable <u>and</u> stem
   ends in two consonants

Neuter I-stems:
nominative singular ends in *-e, -al, -ar*

This is the paradigm for third declension *masculine* and *feminine* declension I-stem nouns.

CASE	SINGULAR	PLURAL
Nominative	nox	noct*ēs*
Genitive	noct*is*	noct*ium*
Dative	noct*ī*	noct*ibus*
Accusative	noct*em*	noct*ēs*
Ablative	nocte	noct*ibus*

This is the paradigm for third declension *neuter* I-stem nouns.

CASE	SINGULAR	PLURAL
Nominative	mare	mar*ia*
Genitive	mar*is*	mar*ium*
Dative	mar*ī*	mar*ibus*
Accusative	mare	mar*ia*
Ablative	mar*ī*	mar*ibus*

It may be helpful to mark the endings on the I-stem chart where they differ from regular third declension nouns.

Lesson Twenty-One Exercises

A. Study the vocabulary. The I-stem nouns are marked with an *.

īnfāns, īnfantis*, m/f	child
adolescens, -entis*, m/f	youth (*adj.*) young, youthful
iuvenis, -is*, m/f	young man or woman (*adj.*) young, youthful
parens, -entis*, m/f	parent
gēns, gentis*, f.	race
genus, -eris, n.	sort, kind, race
homō, hominis, m/f	man, human being
senex, senis, m/f	old person
mātrōna, -ae, f.	married woman, matron
mulier, -eris, f.	woman
marītus, -ī, m.	husband
mors, mortis*, f.	death

Teacher's Note: A substantive (subst.) is a noun taken directly from an adjective. For example, *iuvenis* is an adjective meaning youthful. However, it is frequently used by itself instead of with a noun. Then it appears to be a noun and is treated as a noun for declension and for translation. Hence, *iuvenis* would signal a young person, *iuvenis benignus* would refer to a kind young man, and *iuvenis begnigna* would tell of a kind young woman.

Third declension adjectives are declined like third declension I-stem nouns, but all three genders always have -*ī* in the ablative singular. (See appendix)

B. Solve the riddles. Who is

1. soror mātris?

2. frāter patris?

3. frāter patruī?

4. soror tuae?

5. māter mātris?

6. pater patris?

7. fīlia amitae?

8. fīlius patrī?

9. nōndum (not yet) ambulat?

10. nōn iam ambulat?

11. nōndum marītus, sed nōn infāns est?

12. nōn iam virgō et nōn adolescēns est?

1. amita
2. patruus
3. pater
4. soror
5. avia
6. avus
7. sōbrīna
8. sōbrīnus, or puer patruēlis
9. infāns
10. senex
11. iuvenis, adolescēns
12. uxor, matrōna

C. Here is Psalm 148 as it appears in the Vulgate, the Latin translation of the Bible. Macrons have been added so that the words look more like what you are used to seeing. You will be able to read many parts of it. Look closely at verse 12.

1 Alleluia laudāte Dominum dē caelīs laudāte eum in excelsīs

2 laudāte eum omnēs angelī eius laudāte eum omnēs exercitus eius

3 laudāte eum sol et luna laudāte eum omnēs stellae luminis

4 laudāte eum caelī caelōrum et aquae quae super caelōs sunt

5 laudent nomen Dominī quoniam ipse mandāvit et creata sunt

6 et statuit ea in saeculum et in saeculum praeceptum dedit et nōn praeteribit

7 laudāte Dominum dē terrā draconēs et omnēs abyssī

8 ignis et grandō nix et glaciēs ventus turbō quae facitis sermonem eius

9 montēs et omnēs collēs lignum fructiferum et universae cedrī

10 bēstiae et omnia iumenta reptilia et avēs volantēs

11 regēs terrae et omnēs populī principēs et universī iudicēs terrae

12 iuvenēs et virginēs senēs cum puerīs laudent nomen Dominī

13 quoniam sublime nomen eius solius

14 gloria eius in caelō et in terrā et exaltāvit cornū populī suī laus omnibus sanctīs eius fīliīs Israhel populō adpropinquantī sibi Alleluia

Lesson Twenty-Two

The verb *possum* is an irregular verb in Latin. It is in the same family as *sum*, so it is very easy to learn it's conjugation. *Possum* means *I can*, or *I am able*. We get words like *omnipotent* (able to do all things) from *possum*.

Here is the paradigm of all six tenses of *possum, posse, potuī*.

PRESENT

possum	I can, I am able	possumus	we are able
potes	you are able	potestis	you (pl.) are able
potest	he, she, it is able	possunt	they are able

IMPERFECT

poteram	I was able, I could	poterāmus	we were able
poterās	you were able	poterātis	you (pl.) were able
poterat	he, she, it was able	poterant	they were able

FUTURE

poterō	I will be able	poterimus	we will be able
poteris	you will be able	poteritis	you (pl.) will be able
poterit	he, she, it will be able	poterunt	they will be able

PERFECT

potuī	I was, I have been able	potuimus	we have been able
potuistī	you have been able	potuistis	you (pl.) have been able
potuit	he, she, it has been able	potuērunt	they have been able

PluPerfect

potu*eram*	I had been able	potu*erāmus*	we had been able
potu*erās*	you had been able	potu*erātis*	you (pl.) had been able
potu*erat*	he, she, it had been able	potu*erant*	they had been able

Future Perfect

potu*erō*	I will have been able	potu*erimus*	we will have been able
potu*eris*	you will have been able	potu*eritis*	you will have been able
potu*erit*	he, she, it will have been able	potu*erint*	they will have been able

Lesson Twenty-Two Exercises

A. Many times the verb *possum* is used with an infinitive to convey the idea of *being able to do* something. Write good Latin sentences for these ideas.

1. I can call my brother from the fields.

_____

2. You were able to sail for three years. (Use ablative duration of time)

_____

3. She will be able to carry many rocks with a wagon.

_____

4. We have been able to teach the children many new words.

_____

5. You (pl.) had been able to see the moon and bright stars.

_____

6. They will have been able to hold the infants in (their) laps.

7. The king's son was not able to give a gift to the daughter of the farmer. _____

8. At last the husbands have been able to walk with their wives in the meadow. _____

9. Children are able to flourish with kind, firm parents.

10. Because of his deeds, his words have not been able to stay in their hearts _____

---

1. Frātrem meum ab agrīs possum vocāre.
2. Annīs tribus poterās nāvigāre.
3. Multa saxa plaustrō poterit portāre.
4. Līberīs (indirect object) multa verba nova potuimus docēre.
5. Lunam et stellās clarās potuerātis vidēre.
6. Infāntēs in gremiō potuerint habēre.
7. Fīlius rēgis fīliae (indirect object) agricolae (possessive) dōnum nōn poterat dare.
8. Tandem marītī cum uxōribus in prātō potuērunt ambulāre.
9. Līberī benignīs parentibus firmīs possunt flōrēre.
10. Propter facta sua, dicta in cordibus suīs nōn potuērunt manēre.

Decline a noun from each declension.

fēmina	fēmina, fēminae, fēminae, fēminam, fēminā; fēminae, fēminārum, fēminīs, fēminās, fēminīs
vir	vir, virī, virō, virum, virō; virī, virōrum, virīs, virōs, virīs
verbum	verbum, verbī, verbō, verbum, verbō; verba, verbōrum, verbīs, verba, verbīs
mulier	mulier, mulieris, mulierī, mulierem, muliere; mulierēs, mulierum, mulieribus, mulierēs, mulieribus
caput	caput, capitis, capitī, caput, capite; capita, capitum, capitibus, capita, capitibus
gēns	gēns, gentis, gentī, gentem, gente; gentēs, gentium, gentibus, gentēs, gentibus
animal	animal, animalis, animalī, animal, animalī; animalia, animalium, animalibus, animalia, animalibus

Conjugate a verb from each conjugation. Add *sum* or *possum*.

spectō	spectō, spectās, spectat, spectāmus, spectātis, spectant; spectābam, spectābās, spectābat, spectābāmus, spectābātis, spectābant; spectābō, spectābis, spectābit, spectābimus, spectābitis, spectābunt; spectāvī, spectāvistī, spectāvit, spectāvimus, spectāvistis, spectāvērunt; spectāveram, spectāverās, spectāverat, spectāverāmus, spectāverātis, spectāverant; spectāverō, spectāveris, spectāverit, spectāverimus, spectāveritis, spectāverint
fleō	fleō, flēs flet, flēmus, flētis, flent; flēbam, flēbās, flēbat, flēbāmus, flēbātis, flēbant; flēbō, flēbis, flēbit, flēbimus, flēbitis, flēbunt; flēvī, flēvistī, flēvit, flēvimus, flēvistis, flēvērunt; flēveram, flēverās, flēverat, flēverāmus, flēverātis, flēverant; flēverō, flēveris, flēverit, flēverimus, flēveritis, flēverint
	sum, es, est, sumus, estis, 'sunt; eram, erās, erat, erāmus, erātis, erant; erō, eris, erit, erimus, eritis, erunt; fuī, fuistī, fuit, fuimus, fuistis, fuērunt; fueram, fuerās, fuerat, fuerāmus, fuerātis, fuerant; fuerō, fueris, fuerit, fuerimus, fueritis, fuerint

For *possum*, see pages 135 and 136.

Review adjective vocabulary.

Review adverb vocabulary.

Review prepositions.

Use each preposition in a phrase showing the case ending of the noun.

Optional Unit—Seasons and Weather

Now that we have learned the third declension, we will be able to say and write about many more things than we could before. Many of the words which relate to the world around us come from third declension nouns.

SPRING

vēr, vēris, n.	spring
primō vēre	in the beginning of spring
pluvia, -ae, f.	rain
imber, imbris, m.	shower or storm of rain
nimbus, -ī, m.	cloud
pluit, pluere, (plūvit)	it rains, it rained; to rain
procella, -ae, f.	storm, gale, wind squall
tempestās, tempestātis, f.	storm, tempest
arbor, arboris, f.	tree
flōs, flōris, m.	flower, blossom
folium, -ī, n.	leaf, foliage
rāmus, -ī, m.	bough, branch, twig
vireō, -ēre	to be green, to grow green or healthy
viridis, -e *(adj.)*	green

SUMMER

aestās, aestātis, f.	summer
aestāte novā	at the beginning of summer
sōl, sōlis, m.	sun

AUTUMN

autumnus, -ī, m.	autumn
autumnō vergente	towards the end of autumn

WINTER

hiems, hiemis, f.	winter
hieme	in winter
nix, nivis, f.	snow
niveus, -a, -um	snowy
nivātus, -a, -um	iced, cooled with snow
ningit, ningere, ninxit	it snows

Draw a picture of one of the seasons. (Or draw all of the seasons!) Label all the parts of your picture with a Latin word.

Teacher's Note: As a good review activity, or for building vocabulary, have the students divide into four groups. Have each group write (individually, or one story/group) a story about their season. This is a superb opportunity for practicing adjective/noun agreement and various verb tenses.

Lesson Twenty-Three

Much of our understanding of a language comes from understanding the people who speak the language. How people think, what they do, how they think about past deeds, all these things are part of a people's culture. Many times new words will develop to describe a new tool or action in a culture. For example, when your grandparents were children, the word *fax* was probably not in their dictionary. Now almost everyone knows what a fax machine is or how to send a fax.

In the story we will study in this lesson, we will learn how the meaning of the Latin verb *raptō* was forever set in history. From this word we get words like *rapid*, *rapture*, *rapine*, *rapt*, *raptor*, and *raptorial*.

In this story there are also many words which have to do with fighting or war. Look for the Latin words from which we get *armor*, *belligerent*, *clamor*, *fortitude*, *gladiator*, *military*, *pugnacious*.

Teacher's Note: There is no new grammar in this lesson. The emphasis is building vocabulary and gaining an appreciation for the history of the Roman people.

Lesson Twenty-Three Exercises

A. Study the vocabulary.

eques, -itis, m. – horseman, knight; *pl.* – calvary

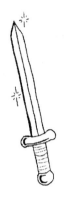

gladius, -ī, m. – sword

onus, -eris, n. – burden, load

rēx, rēgis, m. – king

scūtum, -ī, n. – shield

tempus, -oris, n. – time

arma, -ōrum, n. pl.	arms, weapons
armātus, -a, -um	armed
bellum, -ī, n.	war
cīvis, cīvis* m/f	citizen
cīvitās, -ātis, f.	state
citō *(adv.)*	quickly
fīnitimus, -a, -um	neighbouring
formōsus, -a, -um	beautiful, beautifully formed
medius, -a, -um	middle
mīles, mīlitis, m.	soldier
parō, -āre, -āvī, ātum	prepare
parvulus, -a, -um	very little, very small
pax, pācis, f.	peace
pedes, -itis, m.	foot soldier
urbs, urbis,* f.	city
vox, vōcis, f.	voice

B. Read the story.

ROMULUS ET SABINAE

Rōmulus erat fīlius Martis. Mars erat deus bellī et armōrum. Mīlitēs Rōmānī Martem adōrābant et in Martis ārīs victimās mactābant. Rōmulus igitur mīlitēs et arma vehementer amābat. Urbis Rōmae prīmus rēx erat. Sed sōlum virī urbem habitābant; neque uxōrēs neque sorōrēs habēbant.

Itaque Rōmulus tōtum populum convocāvit, et "O cīvēs," inquit, "nullās fēminās habēmus, sed Sabīnī cīvitātem fīnitimam habitant. Sabīnī fēminās multās et formōsās habent. Sabīnōs igitur cum fēminīs ad lūdōs invītābimus, et virginēs raptābimus."

Rōmānī igitur Sabīnōs ad lūdōs magnōs invītāvērunt. Pax erat inter Rōmānōs et Sabīnōs. Itaque Sabīnī ad lūdōs Rōmānōrum libenter properāvērunt. Nec scūta nec gladiōs nec hastās apportāvērunt. Cum Sabīnīs virginēs multae et formōsae properāvērunt. Sabīnī lūdōs Rōmānōrum spectāvērunt.

In mediīs lūdīs, Rōmānī magnā vōce subitō clāmāvērunt, et ecce! virginēs Sabīnās raptāvērunt et ad casās portāvērunt. Frustrā mātrēs lacrimāvērunt, frustrā virōs in arma incitāvērunt. Rōmānī scūta et gladiōs et hastās habēbant; Sabīnīs nec scūta nec gladiī nec hastae fuērunt.

Maestī igitur et īrātī Sabīnī ad terram Sabīnam properāvērunt. Per tōtam hiemem ibi manēbant et arma diligenter parābant. Via est longa inter Rōmam et terram Sabīnam. Sed tandem Sabīnī, iam armātī, ante portās urbis Rōmae stābant. "O Rōmānī," inquiunt, "prō fīliābus nostrīs, prō sorōribus nostrīs fortiter pugnābimus."

Deinde Sabīnae ē casīs Rōmānōrum passīs capillīs ēvolāvērunt; parvulōs portāvērunt et patribus frātribusque monstrāvērunt. Patrēs frātrēsque suōs multīs lacrimīs ōrāvērunt. "Nunc," inquiunt, "in casīs Rōmānīs laetae et placidae habitāmus; līberōs cārōs habēmus et vehementer amāmus; et Sabīnōs et Rōminōs amāmus. Sī Rōmānī cum Sabīnīs pugnābunt, Rōmānī Sabīnōs, Sabinī Rōmānos necābunt. Tum Sabīnae nec virōs nec patrēs nec frātrēs habēbunt. O patrēs, valēte! nōn iam Sabīnae sed Rōmānae semper erimus fīliae vestrae."

Mars, Martis, m.—Mars, god of war
Rōmulus, -ī, m.—Romulus, the founder of Rome
Sabīnus, -ī, m.—a Sabine, a neighbor of the Romans
Sabīnus, -a, -um—Sabine, belonging to the Sabine tribe
Sabina, -ae, f.—a Sabine woman

Romulus was the son of Mars. Mars was the god of war and of arms (weapons). The Roman soldiers worshipped Mars and offered up victims on the altars of Mars. Romulus, therefore, loved soldiers and weapons very much. He was the first king of the city Rome. But only men were living in the city; they had neither wives nor sisters.

Therefore, Romulus called together all the people and said, "Oh, citizens, we have no women, but the Sabines live in the neighboring state. The Sabines have many (and) beautiful women. Therefore we will invite the Sabines with (their) women to games, and we will seize (their) young women (virgins).

So the Romans invited the Sabines to great games. There was peace between the Romans and the Sabines. Therefore, the Sabines hurried gladly to the Romans' games. Neither shields nor swords nor spears did they bring. Many (and) beautiful young women hurried with the Sabines. The Sabines watched the Romans' games.

In the middle of the games, the Romans suddenly shouted with a great voice, and behold! they seized the Sabine young women and carried them to (their) cottages. In vain the mothers cried, in vain they urged the men (in)to arms. The Romans had shields and swords and spears; there were to the Sabines neither shields, nor swords, nor spears.

Unhappy, therefore, and angry, the Sabines hurried to the Sabine land. Through a whole winter they stayed there and diligently prepared weapons. The way is long between Rome and the Sabine land. But at last the Sabines, now armed, were standing before the gates of the city of Rome. "Oh, Romans," they said, "We will fight bravely for our daughters, for our sisters."

Then the Sabine women (Sabinae) flew out from the cottages of the Romans with hair disheveled; they carried (their) little (ones) and they showed their fathers and brothers. They begged their fathers and brothers with many tears. "Now," they said, "we live happy and calm in the cottages of the Romans; we have dear children and we love (them) greatly; we love both the Sabines and the Romans. If the Romans fight with the Sabines, Romans will kill Sabines, Sabines will kill Romans. Then the Sabine women will have neither men, nor fathers, nor brothers. Oh fathers, be well! we will no longer be Sabines, but Romans, (we will) always (be) your daughters.

C. From the Latin words in the story and how they are used, write your own definitions for the following English words.

evolution _____

filial _____

adore _____

urban _____

habitation _____

civil _____

invitation _____

ludicrous _____

multitude _____

null _____

> Answers will vary.

D. Imagine that you were a Sabine boy or girl at the games. Write a story in Latin from your viewpoint. Use many verb tenses.

_____

_____

_____

_____

_____

_____

Teacher's Note: It can be a wise use of time to have students correct each other's papers. You may give directions to mark mistakes or to correct mistakes. This gives students practice at proofreading and gives final papers with fewer mistakes.

E. Parse the following sentence in the space between the lines. Give the part of speech for every word. Give the case and reason for the case for every noun and adjective. Give the person, number, and tense of every verb.

Deinde Sabīnae ē casīs Rōmānōrum

passīs capillīs ēvolāvērunt;

parvulōs portāvērunt et patribus

frātribusque monstrāvērunt.

Deinde, *adverb*; Sabīnae, *nominative plural, subject*; ē, *preposition*; casīs *ablative plural, object of preposition*; Rōmānōrum, *genitive plural*; passīs, *ablative plural, adjective modifies capillīs*; capillīs, *ablative noun of description or manner*; ēvolāvērunt; *third person, plural, perfect verb*; parvulōs, *accusative plural, substantive noun from the adjective parvulus (translated "little ones")*; portāvērunt, *third person, plural, perfect verb*; et, *conjunction*; patribus, *dative plural, indirect object*; frātribusque, *dative plural, indirect object*, -que *an enclitic ending meaning and*; monstrāvērunt, *third person, plural, perfect verb*.

Lesson Twenty-Four

The *third conjugation* of verbs in Latin is a bit different from the first two conjugations. The infinitive of a third conjugation verb ends with *-ere*. *Dūcō, dūcere, dūxī, ductum* is a third conjugation verb.

Third conjugation verbs form their present stem by dropping *-ō* from the first principal part.

> ## Present Stem (3rd conj.) = First principal part -ō

To add the personal endings (*-ō, -s, -t, -mus, -tis, -nt*) directly to a consonant ending would make the words impossible to say, so we add *-i* or *-u* before the personal endings.

Here is the paradigm for third conjugation present tense verbs.

PRESENT

SINGULAR		PLURAL	
dūc*ō*	I lead	dūc*imus*	we lead
dūc*is*	you lead	dūc*itis*	you (pl.) lead
dūc*it*	he, she, it leads	dūc*unt*	they lead

Teacher's Note: Notice no macron on the first *-e-* in *-ere*. It is very important to distinguish between the second and third conjugation verbs. The easiest way to do this is to memorize the macron or lack of it in the infinitive. If pronounced correctly, the second conjugation infinitive will say "AY-rah," and the third conjugation infinitive will say "ur-rah." Here's one more reason to have students practice vocabulary orally.

The imperfect tense of third conjugation verbs is formed by adding the tense sign *-ēbā-* to the present stem.

Imperfect tense (3rd conj.) = present stem + ēbā + personal endings

Here is the paradigm for third conjugation imperfect tense verbs.

IMPERFECT

SINGULAR		PLURAL	
dūcēbam	I was leading	dūcēbāmus	we were leading
dūcēbās	you were leading	dūcēbātis	you (pl.) were leading
dūcēbat	he, she, it was leading	dūcēbant	they were leading

The future tense is formed by adding the tense sign *-ē-*, but pay close attention to the paradigm, *-ē-* becomes *-a-* in the first person singular and *-e-* before *-t* and *-nt* in the third person.

Future tense (3rd conj.) = present stem + ē + personal endings

Here is the paradigm for third conjugation future tense verbs.

FUTURE

SINGULAR		PLURAL	
dūc*am*	I will lead	dūc*ēmus*	we will lead
dūc*ēs*	you will lead	dūc*ētis*	you (pl.) will lead
dūc*et*	he, she, it will lead	dūc*ent*	they will lead

Teacher's Note: Emphasize -*ē*- as the future tense sign. This is quite different from the -*i*- that is in -*bi*- and *will* and has heretofore been associated with the future tense sign. In this conjugation, -*i*- occurs in the present tense. It sometimes helps the students to think of this as the smallest vowel, the one most easy to fit between the consonants of the present stem and the personal endings.

Lesson Twenty-Four Exercises

A. Study this new vocabulary.

contendō, -ere, -tendī, -tentum	to hasten, to hurry
dēfendō, -ere, -fendī, -fensum	to defend
dīcō, -ere, dīxī, dictum	to say
dūcō, -ere, dūxī, ductum	to lead
fallō, fallere, fefellī, falsum	to deceive, to escape the notice of
incolō, -ere, -uī	to inhabit, to dwell in
legō, -ere, lēgī, lectum	to read
mittō, mittere, mīsī, missum	to send
quaerō, quaerere, quaesīvī, quaesītum	to seek, to look for
regō, -ere, rēxī, rēctum	to rule
scrībō, -ere, scripsī, scriptum	to write
tegō, -ere, texī, tectum	to cover

B. Practice using third conjugation verbs in the three tenses you have learned. Write equivalent phrases in Latin.

1. I will hurry _____

2. We will be able to read _____

3. They defend _____

4. She was deceiving _____

5. We will write _____

6. You (pl.) are seeking _____

7. He will lead _____

8. You (s.) were sending _____

9. They inhabit _____

10. He rules _____

11. They were saying _____

12. It will cover _____

13. We were defending _____

14. Do you (pl.) deceive? _____

15. Will they send? _____

1. Contendam	6. Quaeritis	11. Dīcēbant
2. Poterimus legere	7. Dūcet	12. Teget
3. Dēfendunt	8. Mittēbātis	13. Dēfendēbāmus
4. Fallēbat	9. Incolunt	14. Fallitisne?
5. Scrībēmus	10. Regit	15. Mittentne?

C. Write ten excellent English sentences using words derived from this week's vocabulary.

1. _____
2. _____
3. _____
4. _____
5. _____
6. _____
7. _____
8. _____
9. _____
10. _____

Answers will vary. contend, contentious, defend, defensive, dictate, duke, false, legible, missile, mission, query, regulate, scribe, scripture, tectum

---

DAILY ORAL REVIEW

Conjugate a verb from each of the three conjugations each day.
Decline a noun each day.
Review third declension vocabulary.

Lesson Twenty-Five

The *perfect system of the third conjugation* forms its tenses by the same rules as for the first and second conjugations. To find the perfect stem, drop the *-ī* from the third principal part. To form the perfect tense, add the perfect personal endings. To form the pluperfect tense, add the tense sign *-erā-* and the personal endings. To form the future perfect tense, add the tense sign *-eri-* and the personal endings.

Perfect tense = perfect stem + perfect endings

Perfect stem = third principal part *-ī*

This paradigm is for third conjugation perfect tense verbs.

PERFECT

SINGULAR		PLURAL	
dūxī	I led, I have led	dūximus	we led
dūxistī	you led	dūxistis	you (pl.) led
dūxit	he, she, it led	dūxērunt	they led

PluPerfect tense =
perfect stem + erā + personal endings

This paradigm is for third conjugation pluperfect tense verbs.

PLUPERFECT

SINGULAR		PLURAL	
dūx*eram*	I had led	dūx*erāmus*	we had led
dūx*erās*	you had led	dūx*erātis*	you (pl.) had led
dūx*erat*	he, she, it had led	dūx*erant*	they had led

Future Perfect tense =
perfect stem + eri + personal endings

This paradigm is for third conjugation future perfect tense verbs.

FUTURE PERFECT

SINGULAR		PLURAL	
dūx*erō*	I will have led	dūx*erimus*	we will have led
dūx*eris*	you will have led	dūx*eritis*	you (pl.) will have led
dūx*erit*	he, she, it will have led	dūx*erint*	they will have led

Lesson Twenty-Five Exercises

A. Study this new vocabulary.

agō, agere, ēgī, āctum	to do, to drive
amittō, -ere, amīsī, amissum	to lose, to let go (ā+mittō)
cōgō, -ere, coēgī, coāctum	to collect; to compel (co+agō)
cōnstruō, -ere, -strūxī, -strūctum	to build, to construct
fluō, -ere, flūxī, flūxum	to flow
gerō, gerere, gessī, gestum	to bear, to wear
pōnō, pōnere, posuī, positum	to place, to put
relinquō, -ere, -relīquī, relictum	to leave, to leave behind
surgō, -ere, surrēxī, surrēctum	to rise, to stand up
vincō, vincere, vīcī, victum	to conquer, to defeat

B. Write a story about a past event. Try to use only third declension nouns and third conjugation verbs.

_____

_____

_____

_____

_____

_____

_____

Teacher's Note: The prefix *co-* means *together* or *forcibly*. To drive together (co+agō) is to collect. To drive forcibly (co+agō) is to compel.

Point out to students the differences between the third principal parts of *pōnō* and *possum*. *Fluō* is related to *flumen, -inis,* n. river, and *fluvius, -ī,* m. stream, river.

Lesson Twenty-Six

There is a second group of third conjugation verbs. These are called *third conjugation I-stem verbs*. These verbs are easily identified by their *-ere* infinitive ending and the *-i* in the present stem (which we find for this conjugation by dropping the *-ō* of the first principal part). The present system (present, imperfect, and future tenses) is only a little bit different from the other third conjugation verbs. The perfect system (perfect, pluperfect, and future perfect tenses) follows the rules exactly.

Here is the present system paradigm of a third conjugation I-stem verb.

SINGULAR   PLURAL

PRESENT

faci*ō*	I make, I do	faci*mus*	we make
faci*s*	you make	faci*tis*	you (pl.) make
faci*t*	he, she, it makes	faci*unt*	they make

IMPERFECT

faci*ēbam*	I was making	faci*ēbāmus*	we were making
faci*ēbās*	you were making	faci*ēbātis*	you (pl.) were making
faci*ēbat*	he, she, it was making	faci*ēbant*	they were making

FUTURE

faci*am*	I will make, I will do	faci*ēmus*	we will make
faci*ēs*	you will make	faci*ētis*	you (pl.) will make
faci*et*	he, she, it will make	faci*ent*	they will make

The perfect system of third conjugation verbs looks like this:

	SINGULAR		PLURAL

PERFECT

fēcī	I made, I have made	*fēcimus*	we have made
fēcistī	you have made	*fēcistis*	you (pl.) have made
fēcit	he, she, it has made	*fēciērunt*	they have made

PLUPERFECT

fēceram	I had made, I had done	*fēcerāmus*	we had made
fēcerās	you had made	*fēcerātis*	you (pl.) had made
fēcerat	he, she, it had made	*fēcerant*	they had made

FUTURE PERFECT

fēcerō	I will have made	*fēcerimus* we will have made
fēceris	you will have made	*fēceritis* you (pl.) will have made
fēcerit	he, she, it will have made	*fēcerint* they will have made

Lesson Twenty-Six Exercises

A. Study this new vocabulary.

accipiō, accipere, accēpī, acceptum	to receive, to accept (ad + capiō)
capiō, capere, cēpī, captum	to take, to capture
cōnficiō, -ficere, -fēcī, -fectum	to accomplish, to finish (cum + faciō)
cupiō, cupere, cupīvī, cupītum	to wish, to want, to desire
faciō, facere, fēcī, factum	to make, to do
fugiō, fugere, fūgī, fugitum	to flee, to flee from
iaciō, iacere, iēcī, iactum	to throw, to hurl
incipiō, incipere, incēpī, inceptum	to begin (in + capiō)

B. Tell why?

1. a person would want to capture a confection?
2. Cupid is the symbol of cupidity?
3. a fact is something that is done?
4. a fugitive is always on the run?
5. to eject is to throw away?
6. a plan may be doomed from its inception?
7. a gift may be given, but it must also be accepted?
8. insipid does not come from incipio?

---

1. A *confection* is usually a sweet accomplishment which one would enjoy taking.
2. *Cupid* symbolizes desire for the love of another person.
3. *Fact* comes from faciō, which means *to make, to do.*
4. *Fugitive* comes from fugiō which means *to flee.*
5. *ē+iēcī* combine to mean *thrown away* or *thrown out of.*
6. For success, one must have a good plan *from the beginning.*
7. To accept a gift is to receive it (to one's self).
8. *Insipid* comes from another Latin verb (in + sapiō).

C. Give the Latin phrase which means the same thing as:

1. We shall accomplish   _____
2. He has fled   _____
3. You (pl.) were throwing _____
4. She shall have begun   _____
5. They were capturing   _____
6. He had begun   _____

7. We wish   _____

8. You have accomplished   _____

9. They will capture   _____

10. Am I accepting?   _____

1. Cōnficiēmus	3. Iaciēbātis	5. Capiēbant	7. Cupimus	9. Capient
2. Fūgit	4. Incēperit	6. Incēperat	8. Cōnfēcistī	10. Accipiōne?

D. Read the story for enjoyment. Who had the last laugh?

BACCHUS ET PĪRĀTAE

Inter deōs Rōmānōs agricolae nōn sōlum Cererem sed Bacchum quoque adōrābant et in summō honōre habēbant. Bacchus enim vīnum hominibus dedit et multās artēs docuit. Ad Bacchī ārās agricolae dōna multa, et in prīmīs ūvās vīnumque iūcundum ferēbant, et ārās flōribus laetīs pampinīsque ornābant. Deus igitur vītēs Italicās cūrābat, et ā perīculō dēfendēbat. Formōsus erat deus, et, quod vītēs amābat, capillōs suōs pampinīs saepe ornābat. Nec Italōs Graecōsque sōlum docēbat, sed ad longinquās terrās nāvigābat, aliīsque gentibus vīnum dabat, artēsque rusticās docēbat.

Deus, ubi trāns mare Aegaeum quondam nāvigābat, ad insulam parvam nāvem gubernāvit, et errōribus longīs fessus, sē in ōrā maritimā prostrāvit et somnō placidō corpum animumque recreābat. Mox autem pīrātae quoque, hominēs malī, nāvem ad insulam impulērunt. Ubi iuvenem formōsum in ōrā vidērunt, tum vērō magnō gaudiō, "Ecce!" inquiunt, "nōn sine praedā ad patriam nostram nāvigābimus. Hominem raptābimus et in nāvem furtim impōnēmus, tum cito cum captīvō ad Africam nāvem impellēmus. Africae incolae servōs dēsīderant, et pecūniam multam nōbīs dābunt, sī nōs iuvenem tam pulchrum trādiderimus." Tum pīrātae, malī ignāvīque hominēs, deum raptāvērunt et in nāvem imposuērunt; nec tamen iuvenem fessum ē somnō excitāvērunt.

Ubi autem Bacchus ē somnō sē excitāvit, et undās caeruleās undique vīdit, tum nec īrātus nec perterritus, "Nōn egō," inquit, "stultōs ignāvōsque timeō; mox tamen pīrātae nūmen meum vidēbunt et vehementer timēbunt." Tum ē mediā nāve vītis flōrēbat et in altum ascendēbat. E vīte rāmī ē rāmīs pampinī flōrēbant, et dē summīs rāmīs ūvae purpureae pendēbant. Nōn iam candida erant vēla, sed lūce purpureā fulgēbant.

Ubi nautae vītem mīram in mediā nāve vīdērunt, tum magnō timōre deum spectāvērunt; capillī in capitibus horruērunt. Subitō ex undīs tigrēs leōnēsque saevī in nāvem ascendērunt et in nautās perterritōs cucurrērunt. Pīrātae, terrōris plēnī, ē nāve in mare sē prostrāvērunt. Deinde Iuppiter propter misericordiam hominēs in delphīnīs convertit. Intereā Neptūnus vēla purpurea ventīs secundīs implēvit, et sōlus sub vītium umbrā Bacchus ad terrās longinquās nāvigāvit.

VERBS

horreō, -ēre, -uī, ---- —to shudder, to bristle

impellō, -ere, -pulī, -pulsum—to impel, to drive

trādō, -ere, -didī, -ditum—to hand over, to trade

NOUNS

delphīn, -īnis, n.—dolphin

error, -ōris, m.—wandering

leō, leōnis, m.—lion

misericordia, -ae, f.—pity

nūmen, -inis, n.—a divine power

pampinus, -ī, m.—a vine leaf or tendril

perīculum, -ī, n.—danger

praeda, -ae, f.—plunder

tigris, -is, m/f—tiger

vēlum, -ī, n.—sail

vītis, -is, f.—vine

ADJECTIVES

candidus, -a, -um—white

fessus, -a, -um—tired

saevus, -a, -um—savage, cruel

PRONOUNS

ego—I

nōbīs—to us

nōs—we

Among the Roman gods the farmers not only Ceres but also Bacchus they worshiped and held in highest honor. For Bacchus gave wine to men and taught many arts. To the altars of Bacchus the farmers carried many gifts, and especially grapes and pleasant wine, and they decorated the altars with bright flowers and tendrils of vines. Therefore the god cared for the Italian vines, and defended (them) from danger. The god was handsome, and, because he loved (imperfect for description) vines, he often adorned his hair with tendrils. He was teaching not only the Italians and the Greeks, but he used to sail to faraway lands, and he used to give wine to other peoples and he used to teach the country arts.

Once upon a time when the god was sailing across the Aegean Sea, he turned the small boat toward an island, and tired from long wanderings, he threw (prostrated) himself on the sea-shore and by calm sleep refreshed (recreated) (his) body and mind. Soon, however, pirates also, evil men, drove (their) ship to the island. When they saw the handsome youth on the shore, then truly with great joy, "Behold!" they said, "Not without a prize will we sail to our homeland. We will seize the man and put (the man) secretly in our boat, then quickly with the captive we will sail (drive) the boat to Africa. The inhabitants of Africa want slaves, and they will give to us much money, if we will trade our youth so handsome." The the pirates, evil and ignorant men, seized the god and put (the god) into the boat; nor yet did they wake the tired youth from sleep.

However, when Bacchus woke himself from sleep, and saw the waves and the sky on all sides, then he was neither angry nor afraid. "Not I," he said, "fear foolish and ignorant men; soon however, the pirates will see my divine power and they will fear me very much." Then a vine was growing from the middle of the ship and it grew into the heights. From the vine branches flourished, and from the branches tendrils, and from the highest branches were hanging purple grapes. No longer were the sails white, but they were shining purple.

When the sailors saw the strange vine in the middle of the ship, then they watched the god with great fear; the hairs bristled on (their) heads. Suddenly from the waves savage tigers and lions came up into the ship and they ran into the terrified sailors. The pirates, full of terror, threw themselves from the ship into the sea. Then Jupiter because of pity changed the men into dolphins. Meanwhile Neptune filled the purple sails with favorable winds, and Bacchus alone under the shade of the vine sailed to lands far away.

Optional Unit—Animals

Now that we have learned the third declension, our vocabulary can grow by leaps and bounds. Here are some animal and outdoor words which will be fun to use in compositions.

animal, -lis, n.	animal
arbor, -oris, f.	tree
avis, -is, f.	bird
bōs, bovis, m/f	ox, cow
delphīn, -īnis, n.	dolphin
grex, gregis, m.	flock
leo, leōnis, m.	lion
lux, lūcis, f.	light
mare, maris, n.	sea
mōns, montis, m.	mountain
nāvis, -is, f.	ship
nox, noctis, f.	night
ovis, ovis, m/f	sheep
pastor, -ōris, m.	shepherd
ramus, -ī, m.	branch
tigris, -is, m/f	tiger

Optional Unit—Animals Exercises

A. Tell me in Latin.

1. Three birds are sitting on the branch of a green tree.

2. A lion and a bear are fighting in the forest.

3. The tigers have killed a large white ox.

4. The horses were walking in front of a beautiful wagon.

5. The flock has begun to wander.

6. Animals have not always been fierce.

7. The sheep of the bad shepherd's flock stayed on the mountain all (use *tōtus*) night.

8. The ship sailed quickly through the waters of the sea.

9. It is night, and there is no light on the mountain or the sea.

10. The savage white lion fled from the small, strong man.

These answers are correct, but other answers may also be correct.
1. Avēs trēs in ramō arboris veridis sedent.
2. Leō et ursa in silvā pugnant.
3. Tigrēs magnum bovem album necāvit.
4. Equēs prō plaustrō splendidō ambulābant.
5. Grex incēpit errāre.
6. Animalia nōn semper fera fuērunt.
7. Ovēs gregis pastoris malī in montem nocte totā mānsērunt.
8. Nāvis per aquās maris cito nāvigāvit.
9. Nox est, et lux in monte aut in mare nōn est.
10. Saevus leo albus ē parvō virō validō fūgit.

Paradigm Summaries

First Declension Nouns

	SINGULAR	PLURAL
CASE		
Nominative	puella	puellae
Genitive	puellae	puellārum
Dative	puellae	puellīs
Accusative	puellam	puellās
Ablative	puellā	puellīs

Masculine Second Declension Nouns

Nominative	amīcus	amīcī
Genitive	amīcī	amīcōrum
Dative	amīcō	amīcīs
Accusative	amīcum	amīcōs
Ablative	amīcō	amīcīs

Neuter Second Declension Nouns

Nominative	forum	fora
Genitive	forī	forōrum
Dative	forō	forīs
Accusative	forum	fora
Ablative	forō	forīs

Masculine and Feminine Third Declension Nouns

	SINGULAR	PLURAL
CASE		
Nominative	mīles	mīlitēs
Genitive	mīlitis	mīlitum
Dative	mīlitī	mīlitibus
Accusative	mīlitem	mīlitēs
Ablative	mīlite	mīlitibus

Neuter Third Declension Nouns

Nominative	caput	capita
Genitive	capitis	capitum
Dative	capitī	capitibus
Accusative	caput	capita
Ablative	capite	capitibus

Masculine and Feminine Third Declension I-stem Nouns

	SINGULAR	PLURAL
CASE		
Nominative	nox	noctēs
Genitive	noctis	noctium
Dative	noctī	noctibus
Accusative	noctem	noctēs
Ablative	nocte	noctibus

Neuter Third Declension I-stem Nouns

Nominative	mare	maria
Genitive	maris	marium
Dative	marī	maribus
Accusative	mare	maria
Ablative	marī	maribus

First Conjugation Verbs

SINGULAR   PLURAL

PRESENT

vocō	I call	vocāmus	we call
vocās	you call	vocātis	you (pl.) call
vocat	he, she, it calls	vocant	they call

IMPERFECT

vocābam	I was calling	vocābāmus	we were calling
vocābās	you were calling	vocābātis	you (pl.) were calling
vocābat	he, she, it was calling	vocābant	they were calling

FUTURE

vocābō	I will call	vocābimus	we will call
vocābis	you will call	vocābitis	you (pl.) will call
vocābit	he, she, it will call	vocābunt	they will call

PERFECT

vocāvī	I called, I have called	vocāvimus	we called
vocāvistī	you called	vocāvistis	you (pl.) called
vocāvit	he, she, it called	vocāvērunt	they called

PLUPERFECT

vocāveram	I had called	vocāverāmus	we had called
vocāverās	you had called	vocāverātis	you (pl.) had called
vocāverat	he, she, it had called	vocāverant	they had called

FUTURE PERFECT

vocāverō	I will have called	vocāverimus	we will have called
vocāveris	you will have called	vocāveritis	you (pl.) will have called
vocāverit	he, she, it will have called	vocāverint	they will have called

Second Conjugation Verbs

	SINGULAR		PLURAL

PRESENT

teneō	I hold	tenēmus	we hold
tenēs	you hold	tenētis	you (pl.) hold
tenet	he, she, it holds	tenent	they hold

IMPERFECT

tenēbam	I was holding	tenēbāmus	we were holding
tenēbās	you were holding	tenēbātis	you (pl.) were holding
tenēbat	he, she, it was holding	tenēbant	they were holding

FUTURE

tenēbō	I will hold	tenēbimus	we will hold
tenēbis	you will hold	tenēbitis	you (pl.) will hold
tenēbit	he, she, it will hold	tenēbunt	they will hold

PERFECT

tenuī	I held, I have held	tenuimus	we held
tenuistī	you held	tenuistis	you (pl.) held
tenuit	he, she, it held	tenuērunt	they held

PLUPERFECT

tenueram	I had held	tenuerāmus	we had held
tenuerās	you had held	tenuerātis	you (pl.) had held
tenuerat	he, she, it had held	tenuerant	they had held

FUTURE PERFECT

tenuerō	I will have held	tenuerimus	we will have held
tenueris	you will have held	tenueritis	you (pl.) will have held
tenuerit	he, she, it will have held	tenuerint	they will have held

Third Conjugation Verbs

SINGULAR

PLURAL

PRESENT

dūcō	I lead	dūcimus	we lead
dūcis	you lead	dūcitis	you (pl.) lead
dūcit	he, she, it leads	dūcunt	they lead

IMPERFECT

dūcēbam	I was leading	dūcēbāmus	we were leading
dūcēbās	you were leading	dūcēbātis	you (pl.) were leading
dūcēbat	he, she, it was leading	dūcēbant	they were leading

FUTURE

dūcam	I will lead	dūcēmus	we will lead
dūcēs	you will lead	dūcētis	you (pl.) will lead
dūcet	he, she, it will lead	dūcent	they will lead

PERFECT

dūxī	I led, I have led	dūximus	we led
dūxistī	you led	dūxistis	you (pl.) led
dūxit	he, she, it led	dūxērunt	they led

PLUPERFECT

dūxeram	I had led	dūxerāmus	we had led
dūxerās	you had led	dūxerātis	you (pl.) had led
dūxerat	he, she, it had led	dūxerant	they had led

FUTURE PERFECT

dūxerō	I will have led	dūxerimus	we will have led
dūxeris	you will have led	dūxeritis	you (pl.) will have led
dūxerit	he, she, it will have led	dūxerint	they will have led

Third Conjugation I-stem Verbs

SINGULAR · PLURAL

PRESENT

faciō	I make, I do	facimus	we make
facis	you make	facitis	you (pl.) make
facit	he, she, it make	faciunt	they make

IMPERFECT

faciēbam	I was making	faciēbāmus	we were making
faciēbās	you were making	faciēbātis	you (pl.) were making
faciēbat	he, she, it was making	faciēbant	they were making

FUTURE

faciam	I will make, I will do	faciēmus	we will make
faciēs	you will make	faciētis	you (pl.) will make
faciet	he, she, it will make	facient	they will make

PERFECT

fēcī	I made, I have made	fēcimus	we have made
fēcistī	you have made	fēcistis	you (pl.) have made
fēcit	he, she, it has made	fēcērunt	they have made

PLUPERFECT

fēceram	I had made, I had done	fēcerāmus	we had made
fēcerās	you had made	fēcerātis	you (pl.) had made
fēcerat	he, she, it had made	fēcerant	they had made

FUTURE PERFECT

fēcerō	I will have made	fēcerimus	we will have made
fēceris	you will have made	fēceritis	you (pl.) will have made
fēcerit	he, she, it will have made	fēcerint	they will have made

Irregular Verb - Sum

	SINGULAR		PLURAL

PRESENT

sum	I am	sumus	we are
es	you are	estis	you (pl.) are
est	he, she, it is	sunt	they are

IMPERFECT

eram	I was	erāmus	we were
erās	you were	erātis	you (pl.) were
erat	he, she, it was	erant	they were

FUTURE

erō	I will be	erimus	we will be
eris	you will be	eritis	you (pl.) will be
erit	he, she, it will be	erunt	they will be

PERFECT

fuī	I was, I have been	fuimus	we have been
fuistī	you have been	fuistis	you (pl.) have been
fuit	he, she, it has been	fuērunt	they have been

PLUPERFECT

fueram	I had been	fuerāmus	we had been
fuerās	you had been	fuerātis	you (pl.) had been
fuerat	he, she, it had been	fuerant	they had been

FUTURE PERFECT

fuerō	I will have been	fuerimus	we will have been
fueris	you will have been	fueritis	you will have been
fuerit	he, she, it will have been	fuerint	they will have been

Irregular Verb - Possum

	SINGULAR		PLURAL

PRESENT

possum	I can, I am able	possumus	we are able
potes	you are able	potestis	you (pl.) are able
potest	he, she, it is able	possunt	they are able

IMPERFECT

poteram	I was able, I could	poterāmus	we were able
poterās	you were able	poterātis	you (pl.) were able
poterat	he, she, it was able	poterant	they were able

FUTURE

poterō	I will be able	poterimus	we will be able
poteris	you will be able	poteritis	you (pl.) will be able
poterit	he, she, it will be able	poterunt	they will be able

PERFECT

potuī	I was able, I have been able	potuimus	we have been able
potuistī	you have been able	potuistis	you (pl.) have been able
potuit	he, she, it has been able	potuērunt	they have been able

PLUPERFECT

potueram	I had been able	potuerāmus	we had been able
potuerās	you had been able	potuerātis	you (pl.) had been able
potuerat	he, she, it had been able	potuerant	they had been able

FUTURE PERFECT

potuerō	I will have been able	potuerimus	we will have been able
potueris	you will have been able	potueritis	you will have been able
potuerit	he, she, it will have been able	potuerint	they will have been able

First and Second Declension Adjectives

SINGULAR

	MASCULINE	FEMININE	NEUTER
Nominative	bonus	bona	bonum
Genitive	bonī	bonae	bonī
Dative	bonō	bonae	bonō
Accusative	bonum	bonam	bonum
Ablative	bonō	bonā	bonō

PLURAL

	MASCULINE	FEMININE	NEUTER
Nominative	bonī	bonae	bona
Genitive	bonōrum	bonārum	bonōrum
Dative	bonīs	bonīs	bonīs
Accusative	bonōs	bonās	bona
Ablative	bonīs	bonīs	bonīs

Third Declension Adjectives

SINGULAR

	MASCULINE/FEMININE	NEUTER
Nominative	viridis	viride
Genitive	viridis	viridis
Dative	viridī	viridī
Accusative	viridem	viride
Ablative	viridī	viridī

PLURAL

	MASCULINE/FEMININE	NEUTER
Nominative	viridēs	viridia
Genitive	viridium	viridium
Dative	viridibus	viridibus
Accusative	viridēs	viridia
Ablative	viridibus	viridibus

Latin Vocabulary

Vocabulary–Nouns and Pronouns

A

Africa, -ae, f.,	Africa
ager, -rī, m.,	field, land
agricola, -ae, m.,	farmer
amīcus, -ī, m.,	friend
amita, -ae, f.,	aunt
angulus, -ī, m.,	corner
animus, -ī, m.,	mind
annus, -ī, m.,	year
Apūlia, -ae, f.,	Apulia, a district of Italy
aqua, -ae, f.,	water
āra, -ae, f.,	altar
arbor, -oris, f.,	tree
arma, -ōrum, n. pl.,	arms
armentum, -ī, n.,	herd
ars, artis, f.,	art
audācia, -ae, f.,	boldness
auxilium, auxiliī, n.,	help, aid, assistance
avāritia, -ae, f.,	greed
avia, -ae, f.,	grandmother
avus, -ī, m.,	grandfather

B

Bacchus, -ī, m.,	Bacchus, the god of the vine
bellum, -ī, n.,	war
benevolentia, -ae, f.,	favor, good will
bēstia, -ae, f.,	wild beast
bōs, bovis, m./f.,	ox
bracchium, -ī, n.,	arm
Britannia, -ae, f.,	Britain
Britannus, -ī, m.,	a Briton

C

caelum, -ī, n.,	sky

campus, -ī, m.,	plain
Campus Martius	a strip of land near the Tiber River where the Romans met
capillus, -ī, m.,	hair
captīvus, -ī, m.,	captive
caput, capitis, n.,	head
carmen, -inis, n.,	song
casa, -ae, f.,	house, cottage
causa, -ae, f.,	cause
cēna, -ae, f.,	dinner
Cerēs, Cereris, f.,	Ceres, goddess of the corn
cibus, -ī, m.,	food
cicāda, -ae, f.,	grasshopper
cīvis, -is, m./f.,	citizen
cīvitas, -ātis, f.,	state
clīvus, -ī, m.,	hill
collum, -ī, n.,	neck
columba, -ae, f.,	dove
coma, -ae, f.,	hair
constantia, -ae, f.,	constancy, steadfastness
cōpia, -ae, f.,	supply, abundance
cor, cordis, n.,	heart
corona, -ae, f.,	crown
corpus, -oris, n.,	body
cūnae, -ārum, f. pl.,	cradle
cūra, -ae, f.,	care, worry

D

dea, -ae, f.,	goddess
deus, -ī, m.,	god
dextra, -ae, f.,	right hand
dictum, -ī, n.,	saying
dōnum, -ī, n.,	gift
duodecim	twelve

E

eques, -itis, m.,   horseman, knight
equus, -ī, m.,   horse
error, -ōris, m.,   wandering

F

fābula, -ae, f.,   story, tale, fable
factum, -ī, n.,   deed
fāma, -ae, f.,   fame, talk, rumor, report
familia, -ae, f.,   household
famula, -ae, f.,   a female servant, handmaid
fēmina, -ae, f.,   woman
fenestra, -ae, f.,   window
figūra, -ae, f.,   shape, figure
fīlia, -ae, f.,   daughter
flamma, -ae, f.,   flame
flōs, flōris, m.,   flower
focus, -ī, m.,   hearth
folium, -ī, n.,   leaf
forum, -ī, n.,   forum, market place
fragor, -oris, m.,   crash
frāter, -ris, m.,   brother
frūmentum, -ī, n.,   corn
fulmen, -inis, n.,   lightning, thunder-bolt

G

galea, -ae, f.,   helmet
gaudium, -ī, n.,   joy
gemma, -ae, f.,   gem, jewel
gens, gentis, f.,   race
genu, -ūs, n.,   knee
gladius, -ī, m.,   sword
Graecus, -ī, m.,   a Greek
gremium, -ī, n.,   lap
grex, gregis, m.,   flock

H

harēna, -ae, f.,	beach, sand
hasta, -ae, f.,	spear
herba, -ae, f.,	herb, plant
hiems, -emis, f.,	winter
homo, -inis, m./f.,	a man, human being
honor, -ōris, m.,	honor
hōra, -ae, f.,	hour
Horātius, -ī, m.,	Horatius, a brave Roman

I

ianua, -ae, f.,	door
īra, -ae, f.,	wrath, anger
imber, -ris, m.,	rain, shower
incola, -ae, m.,	inhabitant, resident, settler
infans, -fantis, m./f.,	infant
Inferī, ōrum, m.pl.,	the Lower World
insula, -ae, f.,	island
īra, -ae, f.,	anger
Ītalia, -ae, f.,	Italy
Ītalus, -ī, m.,	an Italian
iter, itineris, n.,	journey
Iūlia, -ae, f.,	Julia
Iūlius, -ī, m.,	Julius, a Roman
Iuppiter, Iovis, m.,	Jupiter, king of the gods
iūs, iūris, n.,	law, justice
iuvencus, -i, m.,	bullock
iuvenis, -is, m./f.,	a young man or woman

L

lacerta, -ae, f.,	lizard
lacrima, -ae, f.,	tear
lacūna, -ae, f.,	pool, pond
latebra, -ae, f.,	hiding place, lair, hideout
lectus, -ī, m.,	bed, couch

liber, -rī, m.,	book
līberī, -ōrum, m. pl.,	children
līlium, -ī, n.,	lily
lingua, -ae, f.,	tongue, language
littera, -ae, f.,	letter (of the alphabet)
litterae, -ārum, f. pl.,	letter (correspondence)
locus, -ī, m.,	place
lūcerna, -ae, f.,	lantern, lamp
lūdus, -ī, m.,	play, school
lūna, -ae, f.,	moon
lupus, -ī, m.,	wolf

M

magister, -rī, m.,	teacher, master
mare, -is, n.,	sea
Mars, Martis, m.,	Mars, god of war
māter, -ris, f.,	mother
memoria, -ae, f.,	memory
mensa, -ae, f.,	table
Metanīra, -ae, f.,	Metanira, mother of Triptolemus
mīles, -itis, m./f.,	soldier
monumentum, -ī, n.,	monument
Mūsae, -ārum, f. pl.,	Muses, nine goddesses

N

nāvicula, -ae, f.,	small ship or boat
nāvis, -is, f.,	ship
nauta, -ae, m.,	sailor
nepos, nepōtis, m.,	grandson
neptis, neptis, f.,	granddaughter
nōs	we
nūmen, -inis, n.,	a divine power
nympha, -ae, f.,	nymph

O

oculus, oculī, m.,	eye
olīva, -ae, f.,	olive
onus, -eris, n.,	burden, load

oppidānus, -ī, m.,	a townsman
oppidum, -ī, n.,	town
ōra, -ae, f.,	coast, shore
ōra maritima, -ae, f.,	sea shore
orbis, -is, m.,	circle
orbis terrārum	the whole world
osculum, -ī, n.,	kiss

P

palla, -ae, f.,	cloak
pampinus, -ī, m.,	a vine leaf or tendril
parens, -entis, m./f.,	parent
pater, -ris, m.,	father
patria, -ae, f.,	fatherland, country
patruus, -ī, m.,	uncle
pectus, -oris, n.,	breast
paenīnsula, -ae, f.,	peninsula
pax, pācis, f.,	peace
pecūnia, -ae, f.,	money, reward
perīculum, -ī, n.,	danger
Persephonē, -ēs, f.,	Persephone, daughter of Ceres
pēs, pedis, m.,	foot
pīrāta, -ae, f.,	pirate
pictūra, -ae, f.,	picture
plaustrum, -ī, n.,	wagon
Plūto, -ōnis; m.,	Pluto, king of the Underworld
poēta, -ae, m.,	poet
poena, -ae, f.,	penalty, punishment
pōmum, -ī, n.,	fruit, apple
pontus, -ī, m.,	sea
populus, -ī, m.,	people, nation
porta, -ae, f.,	door, gate
praeda, -ae, f.,	plunder
prandium, -ī, n.,	lunch
prātum, -ī, n.,	meadow
proelium, proeliī, n.,	battle, fight
prōra, -ae, f.,	prow

prōvincia, -ae, f.,	province
puella, -ae, f.,	girl
puer, -ī, m.,	boy

Q

Quirīnus, -ī, m.,	Quirinus, the name of Romulus after he was deified
Quirītēs, -ium, m.pl.,	Quirites, a name of the Roman people

R

rēgīna, -ae, f.,	queen
rēgia, -ae, f.,	palace, royal residence
regio, -ōnis, f.,	region, district
regnum, -ī, n.,	kingdom
rex, rēgis, m.,	king
rīpa, -ae, f.,	bank (of a river)
Rōma, -ae, f.,	Rome
Rōmānus, -ī, m.,	a Roman
Rōmulus, -ī, m.,	Romulus, the founder of Rome
rosa, -ae, f.,	rose
rota, -ae, f.,	wheel
ruīna, -ae, f.,	ruin
rūs, rūris, n.,	country

S

Sabīnus, -ī, m.,	a Sabine, neighbor of the Romans
sagitta, -ae, f.,	arrow
sapientia, -ae, f.,	wisdom
saxum, -ī, n.,	rock, stone
schola, -ae, f.,	school
scūtum, -ī, n.,	shield
sē	himself, etc (*reflexive pronoun*)
semita, -ae, f.,	path
servus, -ī, m.,	slave
Sicilia, -ae, f.,	Sicily
silva, -ae, f.,	forest, wood

sinistra, -ae, f.,	left hand
sinistrum, -ī, n.,	left side
somnus, -ī, m.,	sleep
soror, -ōris, f.,	sister
stella, -ae, f.,	star

T

tabula, -ae, f.,	tablet
templum, -ī, n.,	temple
tempus, -oris, n.,	time
tenebrae, -ārum, f. pl.,	shadows, darkness
terra, -ae, f.,	land, earth, ground
Tiberis, -is, m.,	the Tiber River
timor, -ōris, m.,	fear
toga, -ae, f.,	toga, the dress of the Roman men
Triptolemus, -ī, m.,	Triptolemus, the inventor of agriculture
tunica, -ae, f.,	tunic
turba, -ae, f.,	crowd, throng, mob

U

umbra, -ae, f.,	shade, shadow, ghost
unda, -ae, f.,	wave
urbs, urbis, f.,	city
ursa, -ae, f.,	bear
ursus, -ī, m.,	bear
ūva, -ae, f.,	grape
uxor, -ōris, f.,	wife

V

vallis, -is, f.,	valley
ventus, -ī, m.,	wind
verbum, -ī, n.,	word
via, -ae, f.,	street, road, highway, way, journey
victima, -ae, f.,	victim
villa, -ae, f.,	villa, house
vīnea, -ae, f.,	vineyard

vīnum, -ī, n.,	wine
vir, -ī, m.,	man, hero, husband
virgo, -inis, f.,	virgin
vīta, -ae, f.,	life
vītis, -is, f.,	vine
vōs	you (*plural*)
vox, vōcis, f.,	voice

Vocabulary–Adjectives and Adverbs

A

ā sinistrā	on the left hand
adhūc	still, yet
adolescens, adolescentis	young, just grown up
Aegaeus, Aegaea, Aegaeum	Aegaean
aeger, aegra, aegrum	sick
albus, alba, album	white
alius, alia, alium	another
altus, alta, altum	high, deep
amoenus, amoena, amoenum	pleasant, lovely
apertus, aperta, apertum	open
armātus, armāta, armātum	armed

B

bene	well
benignus, benigna, benignum	kind
bonus, bona, bonum	good
Britannicus, Britannica, Britannicum	British

C

caeruleus, caerulea, caeruleum	blue
cārus, cāra, cārum	dear
celeriter	quickly
cēteri, cēterae, cētera	the rest
citō	quickly
cotīdiē	every day
croceus, crocea, croceum	yellow
crūdēliter	cruelly

D

deinde	then, next
dīligenter	carefully
dēnsus, dēnsa, dēnsum	thick, dense
diū	for a long time
dīvīnus, dīvīna, dīvīnum	divine

E

etiam	even, also
extrēmus, extrēma, extrēmum	extreme, farthest

F

ferendus, ferenda, ferendum	bearable, to be borne
ferus, fera, ferum	fierce
fessus, fessa, fessum	tired
fīdus, fīda, fīdum	faithful
fīnitimus, fīnitima, fīnitimum	neighbouring
firmus, firma, firmum	firm, strong
flāvus, flāva, flāvum	yellow, yellow-haired
formōsus, formōsa, formōsum	beautiful
fortasse	perhaps
forte	by chance
fortiter	bravely
frustrā	in vain
furtim	secretly, stealthily

G

grātus, grāta, grātum	pleasing
gelidus, gelida, gelidum	cold
grātus, grāta, grātum	pleasant, welcome

H

herbōsus, herbōsa, herbōsum	grassy
hic	here

I

iam	now, already
ibi	there
ignāvus, ignāva, ignāvum	cowardly, base
ignōtus, ignōta, ignōtum	unknown
impavidus, impavida, impavidum	fearless
industrius, industria, industrium	industrious
intereā	meanwhile

īrātus, īrāta, īrātum	angry
iterum	again
iūcundus, iūcunda, iūcundum	pleasant

L

laetus, laeta, laetum	happy, glad
lātus, lāta, lātum	wide, broad
lībenter	willingly, gladly
līberus, lībera, līberum	free
longinquus, longinqua, longinquum	distant
longus, longa, longum	long

M

maestus, maesta, maestum	sad
magnus, magna, magnum	great, large
malus, mala, malum	bad, evil, wicked
māne	in the morning
Martius, Martia, Martium	belonging to Mars
medius, media, medium	middle
meus, mea, meum	my
mīrus, mīra, mīrum	wonderful
miser, misera, miserum	unhappy
mox	soon
multus, multa, multum	many, much

N

nōn	not
nōn iam	no longer
noster, nostra, nostrum	our
nōtus, nōta, nōtum	well known, famous
nullus, nulla, nullum	no
nunc	now
nusquam	nowhere

O

ōlim	one day, once upon a time

P

placidus, placida, placidum	calm
parātus, parāta, parātum	ready
parvulus, parvula, parvulum	little
parvus, parva, parvum	small, little
passim	everywhere
passus, passa, passum	spread out, dishevelled
perterritus, perterrita, perterritum	frightened
piger, pigra, pigrum	lazy
plēnus, plēna, plēnum	full
prīmus, prīma, prīmum	first
praeclārus, praeclāra, praeclārum	splendid, famous
procul	far
profundus, profunda, profundum	deep
pulcher, pulchra, pulchrum	beautiful
purpureus, purpurea, purpureum	purple

Q

quiētus, quiēta, quiētum	quiet
quondam	once upon a time
quoque	also

R

raucus, rauca, raucum	noisy, raucous
rectus, recta, rectum	straight, right
Rōmānus, Rōmāna, Rōmānum	Roman
rotundus, rotunda, rotundum	round
ruber, rubra, rubrum	red
rusticus, rustica, rusticum	rustic, belonging to the country

S

Sabīnus, Sabīna, Sabīnum	Sabine
saepe	often
saevus, saeva, saevum	savage, cruel
satis	enough
scelerātus, scelerāta, scelerātum	wicked
semper	always
serēnus, serēna, serēnum	calm

sollicitus, sollicita, sollicitum	anxious
sōlus, sōla, sōlum	alone, only
splendidus, splendida, splendidum	splendid
statim	at once
stultus, stulta, stultum	foolish
subitō	suddenly
summus, summa, summum	highest, very great
suus, sua, suum	his own (*reflexive adjective*)

T

tandem	at last
tōtus, tōta, tōtum	whole
tum	then
tuus, tua, tuum	thy, your (*singular*)

U

ubi	where, when (*relative adverb*)
undique	on every side, from all sides
ūnus, ūna, ūnum	one

V

validus, valida, validum	strong
vehementer	exceedingly, very much
vērō	indeed
vester, vestra, vestrum	your (*plural*)

Vocabulary–Verbs

A

accusō, -āre, -āvī, -ātum	to accuse, to blame
adōrō, -āre, āvī, -ātum	to worship
aedificō, -āre, āvī, -ātum	to build
agitō, -āre, -āvī, -ātum	to drive, to arouse, to disturb
ambulō, -āre, -āvī, -ātum	to walk
amō, -āre, -āvī, -ātum	to love
apportō, -āre, -āvī, -ātum	to bring, to take
appropinquō, -āre, -āvī, -ātum	to approach, to draw near
arō, -āre, -āvī, -ātum	to plough

C

cantō, -āre, -āvī, -ātum	to sing
cēlō, -āre, -āvī, -ātum	to hide, to conceal
clāmō, -āre, -āvī, -ātum	to shout, to cry out
conciliō, -āre, - āvī, -ātum	to win over
conservō, -āre, -āvī, -ātum	to save, to preserve
contendō, -ere, -tendī, -tentum	to hasten
convocō, -āre, -āvī, -ātum	to call together
culpō, -āre, -āvī, -ātum	to blame
cūrō, -āre, -āvī, -ātum	to take care of

D

dēfendō, -ere, -fendī, -fensum	to defend
dēlectō, -āre, -āvī, -ātum	to delight
dēmonstrō, -āre, -āvī, -ātum	to point out, to show
dēsiderō, -āre, -āvī, -ātum	to desire, to want
dō, dare, dedī, datum	to give
doceō, -ere, docuī, doctum	to teach
dormītō, -āre, -āvī, -ātum	to sleep

E

ecce	behold
errō, -āre, -āvī, -ātum	to err, to wander, to be mistaken
excidō, -ere, -cīdī, -cīsum	to cut down, to destroy

exclāmō, -āre, -āvī, -ātum   to exclaim
exerceō, -ere, -cuī, -citum   to exercise
expectō, -āre, -āvī, -ātum   to expect, to wait for
explorō, -āre, -āvī, -ātum   to explore
ēvocō, -āre, -āvī, -ātum   to evoke, to call forth
ēvolō, -āre, -āvī, -ātum   to fly out

F

fallō, -ere, fefelli, falsum   to deceive, to escape the notice of
ferō, ferre, tuli, lātum   to bear, to carry
fleō, -ēre, flēvī, flētum   to weep
flōreō, -ēre, -ruī   to flourish, to flower
fugō, -āre, -āvī, -ātum   to put to flight
fulgeō, -ēre, fulsī   to shine

G

gubernō, -āre, -āvī, -ātum   to govern, to steer

H

habeō, -ēre, -buī, -bitum   to have, to hold
habitō, -āre, -āvī, -ātum   to dwell, to live in, to inhabit
horreō, -ēre, -uī, -itum   to shudder, to bristle

I

iaceō, -ēre, -cuī, -citum   to lie
iaceo, iacere, iēcī, iactum   to lay, to throw
iactō, -āre, -āvī, -ātum   to throw, to toss
impellō, -ēre, -pulī, -pulsum   to impel, to drive
impōnō, -ēre, -posuī, -positum   to put in or on
incitō, -āre, -āvī, -ātum   to urge on
incolō, -ēre, -uī   to inhabit, to dwell in
inquit   said he
inquiunt   said they
invītō, -āre, -āvī, -ātum   to invite
iuvō, iuvāre, iūvī, iūtum   to help, to aid

L

labōrō, -āre, -āvī, -ātum	to work
lacrimō, -āre, -āvī, -ātum	to weep
laudō, -āre, -āvī, -ātum	to praise
laxō, -āre, -āvī, -ātum	to relax, to loosen
legō, -ēre, lēgī, lectum	to read

M

mactō, -āre, -āvī, -ātum	to offer up, to slay
mandō, -āre, -āvī, -ātum	to entrust
maneō, -ēre, mansī, mansum	to remain
monstrō, -āre, -āvī, -ātum	to show, to point out
mutō, -āre, -āvī, -ātum	to change, to alter

N

nārrō, -āre, -āvī, -ātum	to narrate, to tell
natō, -āre, -āvī, -ātum	to swim
navigō, -āre, -āvī, -ātum	to sail
necō, -āre, -āvī, -ātum	to kill
nominō, -āre, -āvī, -ātum	to name, to call

O

occupō, -āre, -āvī, -ātum	to seize, to occupy
ornō, -āre, -āvī, -ātum	to adorn, to equip
orō, -āre, -āvī, -ātum	to ask for
oppugnō, -āre, -āvī, -ātum	to attack

P

parō, -āre, -āvī, -ātum	to prepare
perterreō, -ēre, -uī, -itum	to frighten
portō, -āre, -āvī, -ātum	to carry
postulō, -āre, -āvī, -ātum	to demand
properō, -āre, -āvī, -ātum	to hasten, to hurry
prosternō, -ere, -strāvī, -strātum	to prostrate, to overthrow
pugnō, -āre, -āvī, -ātum	to fight

Q

quaerō, -ere, -sīvī, -sītum	to seek, to look for

R

raptō, -āre, -āvī, -ātum	to snatch, to seize
recitō, -āre, -āvī, -ātum	to read aloud, to recite
recreō, -āre, -āvī, -ātum	to refresh
recūsō, -āre, -āvī, -ātum	to refuse
regnō, -āre, -āvī, -ātum	to reign
rogō, -āre, -āvī, -ātum	to ask

S

saltō, -āre, -āvī, -ātum	to dance
scibō, -ēre, scripsi, scriptum	to write
sedeō, -ēre, sēdī, sessum	to sit
servō, -āre, -āvī, -ātum	to save, to keep
spectō, -āre, -āvī, -ātum	to look at, to watch
stō, stare, stetī, statum	to stand
sum, esse, fuī, futurus	to be

T

tardō, -āre, -āvī, -ātum	to slow down, to delay
tegō, -ēre, texī, tectum	to cover
temptō, -āre, -āvī, -ātum	to try, to attempt
teneō, -ēre, tenuī, tentum	to hold
timeō, -ēre, -uī	to fear
trādō, -ēre, -idī, -itum	to hand over

V

valē, *pl.* valēte	goodbye
valeō, -ēre, valuī	I am well
videō, -ēre, vīdī, vīsum	to see
vigilō, -āre, -āvī, -ātum	to be on guard, to stand watch
vitō, -āre, -āvī, -ātum	to avoid, to shun
vocō, -āre, -āvī, -ātum	to call
volō, -āre, -āvī, -ātum	to fly
vulnerō, -āre, -āvī, -ātum	to wound

Vocabulary—Conjunctions and Prepositions

A

ā, ab	by, from
ad	to, towards
ante	before
autem	but

C

cum	with

E

et	and
et . . . et	both . . . and
ē, ex	out of, from

D

dē	down from, concerning

I

igiter	therefore
in *(with ablative)*	in, on
in *(with accusative)*	into, onto
in prīmis	especially
inter	between, among
ita	so, thus
itaque	and so

N

nam	for
nec	and not, nor
neque	and not, nor

P

per	through, among
post	after

prō	for, on behalf of
prope	near
propter	on account of

Q

-que	and
quia	because
quod	because

S

sed	but
sī	if
sine	without

T

tam	so
tamen	however
trans	across

Appendix: Patterns for Diagraming Sentences

If one has never diagramed a sentence, the thought of it may at first be overwhelming. However, as all good students of Latin know, a sentence is merely the sum of its parts! In this brief help, I will show the steps of diagraming.

Even in upper level translation work, it is sometimes helpful to diagram Latin sentences to discover the author's style or intent. This is not an exhaustive list of the kinds of sentences one may write or read. It will be quite sufficient for the scope of this text.

Beginning with short segments of sentences, drawn with generic labels and followed by examples of phrases which would be diagramed in this way, the patterns progress through diagraming sentences of varying difficulty.

These patterns will serve as guides for many other combinations of words and phrases. At this point the students will not be reading compound sentences or sentences with dependent clauses. For older students who wish to pursue this, reference *Warriner's English Grammar and Composition, Complete Course,* ©1986, Harcourt Brace Jovanovich, Inc.

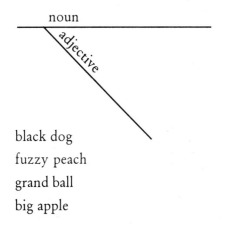

black dog
fuzzy peach
grand ball
big apple

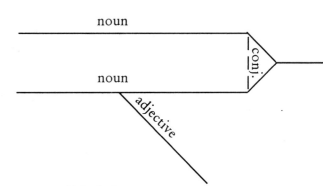

cat and black dog
worm and fuzzy peach
feast and grand ball
sandwich and big apple

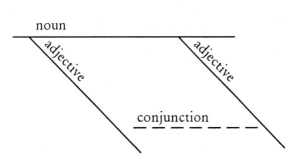

large but bubbly pot
red and green tree
smooth and shiny plum
animals, great or small

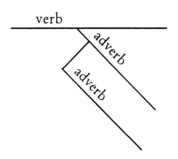

jumped very high
fell rather quickly
came more timidly
thought more cunningly

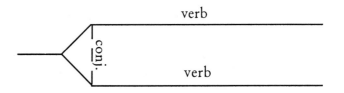

laughed and called
leaped but fell
run or walk
clanged and rattled

subject noun/pronoun	verb

George ran.
Abe was sitting.
Jane has talked.
They were thinking.

subject (noun)	linking verb	predicate nominative

Hannah is hostess.
John is president.
Dogs are pets.
Flowers become fruit.
Trains are transporters.

subject (noun)	linking verb	predicate adjective

Geraniums are lovely.
James seems grumpy.
Tabithah grows weary.
Summer is hot.
God is faithful.

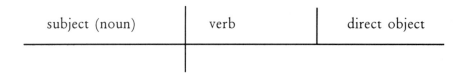

Jim drives trucks.
George has raised corn.
Nina watches children.
Babies drink milk.
They were buying cars.

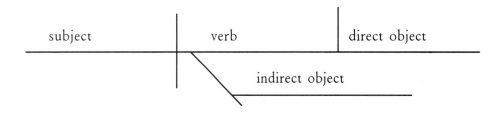

Jane tells children stories.
Harriet gives doctors reports.
Parents give sons direction.
Chad shows monkeys tricks.
Glenda told Sally riddles.

Any parts of the sentence may be compound or may have modifiers.

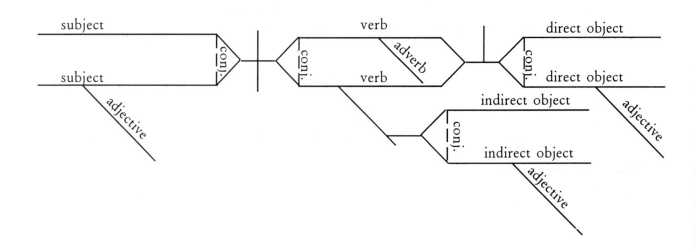

A more complex modifier than an adjective or adverb is the prepositional phrase which may modify nouns, verbs, adjectives, or adverbs.

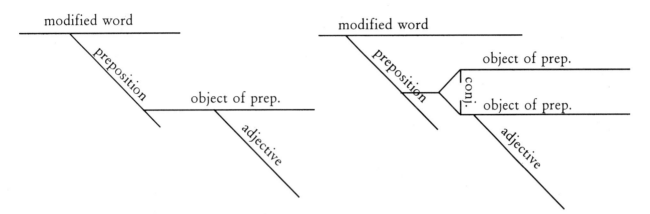

people in glass houses
was going to the* store
long in the tooth
far from the shore
away in the distance

people in elevators and glass houses
had gone to market and the* station
wise in folklore and the weather
hidden by shadows and dark clouds

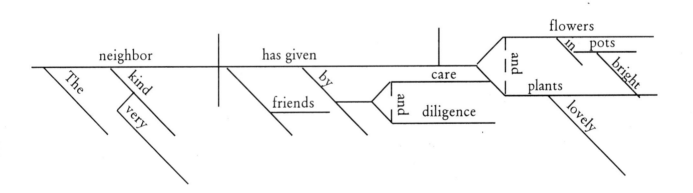

The very kind neighbor has given friends flowers in bright pots and lovely plants by care and diligence.

* The articles, *a*, *an*, and *the* are diagramed as adjectives.